THREE THINGS MATTER MOST

Linking Time, Relationships, and Money

Brett Atlas

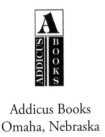

Addicus Books
Omaha, Nebraska

An Addicus Nonfiction Book

ISBN: 978-1-950091-54-6

Typography and cover by Jack Kusler

Library of Congress Cataloging-in-Publication Data

Names: Atlas, Brett, 1973–author.
Title: Three things matter most : linking time, relationships, and money / Brett Atlas.
Description: Omaha, Nebraska : Addicus Books, [2021] | Includes bibliographical references.
Identifiers: LCCN 2021019383 | ISBN 9781950091546 (trade paperback)
Subjects: LCSH: Time management. | Interpersonal relations. | Finance, Personal. | Conduct of life. | Success. | Happiness.
Classification: LCC BF637.T5 A85 2021 | DDC 640/.43—dc23
LC record available at https://lccn.loc.gov/2021019383

Addicus Books, Inc.
P.O. Box 45327
Omaha, Nebraska 68145
AddicusBooks.com
Printed in the United States of America
10 9 8 7 6 5 4 3 2 1

To the memory of my dad,
whom I miss every day.
In honor of my mom,
who was always proud of me,
whether I deserved it or not.
For my wife, Stacey, my North Star.
And to our three children:
Zach, Noah, and Marley.
You were in my mind every word I typed.

Contents

Acknowledgments

The challenge with providing thanks and acknowledgement is that by recognizing some individuals, you inadvertently exclude others. There are more people deserving of my appreciation than I have room for in these pages. Regardless, I will attempt to target my gratitude to those directly or indirectly responsible for this book. If you don't see your name below, it doesn't mean I don't love you.

To Stacey, Zach, Noah, and Marley for giving my life its true joy and purpose. Each of you is a gift, and I couldn't have written this book without the many ways you continue to inspire me.

To Mom and Dad not only for giving me your love and your time but for instilling in me the core values I treasure most. I was incredibly lucky to have you as my parents.

To my brother, James, and my sister, Samantha, for always making me feel like we're all still home together, even though we're hundreds of miles apart.

To Carl and Zoe for your unconditional love and support. I would not be the person I am today without your guidance, influence, and generosity. Together with Carin (who also contributed some wonderful edits), Andrew, Rachel, and Ryan, you've blurred out the word "in-law."

To my publisher, Rod Colvin of Addicus Books. You believed in this book from day one and were a true partner in the process. Nobody else would have been as emotionally invested or as supportive as you have been. Thanks to my editor, Susan Adams, for a master class in editing. I will never be able to read a book the same way again without considering how much impact the editor likely had on the finished product. Thanks also to Jack Kusler for the design, layout, and spirit of partnership.

To Scott Kroeger not only for being an invaluable part of my life but for whipping the original manuscript into shape. Your insights and willingness to call me out made this a much stronger and more authentic read.

To my friends and fellow authors Brian Haara, Fred Minnick, David Jennings, and Harlan Cohen, thank you for all the time, encouragement, suggestions, and feedback. You helped me get this across the finish line.

To Rich Friedman, my second brother, thank you for always being there no matter the miles between us. You've been on this journey with me since we were kids and your input helped me find the right home for the manuscript.

To Andy Ruback, one of my first friends in Omaha and one of the people who knows me best. You have helped me to make sense of the wild swings of life and provided valuable feedback on my writing.

To my Forum Group: Andy Ruback, Brian Nogg, Jason Epstein, Jeffrey Schrager, Jim Glazer, Jonathan Rockman, Marc Scheer, and Scott Meyerson. Thank you for helping me better understand myself over the years and for always being my personal board of directors. I wouldn't have been able to clarify and articulate several of these ideas without your counsel.

Introduction

One day, a giant ship's engine failed. The ship's owner brought in one mechanic after another, but none of them could locate the problem. One of the mechanics suggested the name of an old man who had been fixing ships his entire life. The ship's owner located the old man and brought him in to take a look at the broken engine.

The old man arrived with a large bag of tools and immediately set to work. He inspected the engine carefully, looking it over from top to bottom. The ship's owner watched the old man carefully, hoping he would find the answer.

After a little while, the old man reached into his bag and pulled out a small hammer. He gently tapped something on the engine, and it immediately lurched to life. The engine was fixed!

A week later, the ship's owner received a bill from the old man for $10,000.

"What?!" the owner exclaimed, "He hardly did anything!" The ship's owner sent the old man a note saying, "Please send me an itemized bill for the engine repair." In response, he received a bill from the old man, which read:

Tapping with a hammer $2.00
Knowing where to tap $9,998.00

All the knowledge and skills in the world are not enough without the wisdom to implement them. When it comes to the three things that matter most, knowing where to tap is the secret to a life of happiness and meaning. I'm going to teach you how.

Three Is a Magic Number.

—SCHOOLHOUSE ROCK!
SATURDAY MORNING
TELEVISION SERIES

This book began as a collection of Post-it notes, journal entries, and e-mails. I wanted to develop a repository of generational wisdom for my kids to have. I wanted them to be able to read it at different stages in their lives. I wanted them to have the benefit of all I had learned, even if I was no longer around to share it with them. I've read hundreds of books over the years in my search for life's answers. What I've discovered is three really big ideas, common to all of us, yet ignored by so many. As the old man who fixed the ship demonstrated, experience and wisdom are valuable commodities. They come from a desire to learn and improve ourselves. They come from making our time here worthwhile. I hope to be able to show you areas in your life where you can tap your hammer.

I realize it may seem a bit unusual to begin a book with the author's biographical information. However, I am sharing such information about myself because I believe it will provide better context for the points I make throughout the book. If you know a little bit about me, then you'll see where the ideas came from and why it was so important for me to share them.

I was born in Chicago in 1973 and grew up in the northern suburbs as the middle one of three kids. I have an older brother, James, and a younger sister, Samantha.

Introduction

Our parents were divorced when I was eight years old. We continued living with our mom, but our dad was never far away. When I was eleven, he married a woman with two children of her own. He and my stepmother were actively involved in raising us. They often included my mom in dinners, events, and the occasional vacation. As a result, we children often had three parents around. My mom remained single until she remarried in 2003, which was the same year I moved to Omaha. I was thirty at the time and my wife, Stacey, was pregnant with the first of our three kids. Nebraska is the third state I've lived in. Coincidence perhaps, but it seems like a lot of threes to me.

Back to my childhood. My parents' divorce had a big impact on me, as it does for most young children. A parent leaving the house creates insecurity, and this can wreck a kid's confidence during a critical developmental stage. In addition, my stepmother's behavior often resembled that of an older child rather than of a parent. Love and support seldom felt unconditional. Though I didn't always appreciate it at the time, therapy later taught me at an early age how to better understand my feelings and develop self-awareness. This became extremely useful in my recurring role as the family glue, in which I maneuvered behind the scenes in an effort to keep the fragile pieces from breaking apart. I became hypersensitive to physical cues and highly attuned to what others were feeling.

By necessity, I developed a solid ability to read people and find all the little buttons to push to keep everyone happy. In retrospect, it seems an unfair burden for a child to carry, but I derived a great sense of purpose feeling that I was the one person who could solve the family's problems. Despite the residual psychological wires I've worked to untangle over the years, the one skill I could always lean on was the ability to quickly figure people out.

I did not particularly enjoy my early schooling, but I loved learning outside of it. I was drawn to any kind of mystery and the subsequent search for the answers. I read all the mystery and detective books my mom could find. My dad bought us every new computer adventure game they made—the classic ones that required solving puzzles by typing commands like "Go North" and "Pick Lock." Every Sunday morning, he would share a new logic riddle with us kids, and we had a week to come up with the answer. This early passion for uncovering the secrets in life is what eventually drove my quest to identify the three things that matter most.

My older brother, James, was always popular, but I struggled socially for many years. I allowed myself to feel unworthy around popular kids, and was ostracized as a result. I have a painful memory of my mom walking me into a kid's birthday party and the whole room booing my arrival. Things began to change when I got to middle school. Motivated by James's athletic success, I began working out and eating better. Aided by a timely growth spurt, things had turned around by eighth grade. Girls were now paying attention to me, and I was suddenly also being accepted by guys who had been jerks to me for years.

My deep-seated insecurities were like a rope tied tightly around my swelling ego. I felt like an imposter at times, like I didn't belong, which negatively impacted my confidence and my relationships for years after. When people are popular from a young age, I suspect they have no frame of reference for what it's like to be excluded or made to feel inferior. For me, though, it often felt foreign being part of the "cool" crowd, despite spending plenty of time with them. Even when I eventually became a captain of the varsity football team, I still didn't really feel popular. I had been on both sides of the social divide, and I was still the same person inside. It took me a long time to stop questioning whether or not I deserved to be somewhere.

Introduction

For years, I almost felt like the Wizard of Oz. People saw something confident and put-together on the outside that was actually controlled by a nervous little man inside. Though I couldn't completely eliminate my negative feelings, I developed the self-awareness to understand how I appeared to others. I learned that often the difference between being accepted or ignored turned largely on how I presented myself. It was one of the great puzzles I had solved about relationships. If people could be so easily tricked about how I feel or what I'm really like, then how much should I really care about what they think? Discovering these insights not only gave me the confidence to become who I am but also made me passionate to share them with other people who might also benefit from them.

My career has also been an evolving journey with unexpected leaps and falls. I've worked fairly consistently since I was pretty young. When I was eight, I cleaned bathrooms and swept the warehouse at my dad's swimming pool company after summer camp. It was basically like being paid to go to day care, only the toys were copy machines and the jungle gyms were stacked boxes of files. I loved spending time with my dad and watching him run his businesses.

In middle school I graduated to making concrete coping pieces for swimming pools. Once I could drive, I sold clothing at a retail store and delivered pizzas. Pro tip: Your delivery guy can see what's going on in your house and your hotel room, so be aware (especially late at night)! The most physically demanding job I ever had was cleaning swimming pools, which I did for three straight summers after high school. Being the pool boy isn't what it looks like in the movies.

I joined my two best friends at the University of Kansas, where I served as the president of my fraternity and graduated in 1995 with a business degree. When I told my dad freshman year that I was considering majoring in political science, he sarcastically asked, "What are you going to do, open a chain of 'poli-sci' stores?" He always wanted the best for us, but he also felt he knew what that was. Because I had already decided I was going to work with him eventually, I listened to everything he said and ignored other paths I might have explored. When he told me that I should go to law school because the education alone is invaluable, I came home after graduation to attend the John Marshall Law School.

Shortly before leaving Kansas, Lisa, a friend of mine from Omaha, gave me the phone number of her good friend who was entering her senior year at Northwestern, just up the road from my home. I hadn't yet gotten around to calling when, after about two weeks, my phone rang.

"Hi," the girl said, "this is Stacey, Lisa's friend from Omaha."

That was the first of many long phone calls, and everything just clicked from the beginning. We didn't start dating right away, because I knew she was special and I was worried I would screw it all up. I remember telling both my brother and my sister pretty early on that I knew this was the girl I would marry. Starting out as friends gave me the opportunity to really get to know Stacey and for her to get to know me. She does not get nearly the credit she deserves for how much she has improved me as a person or for what she put up with along the way. I sometimes wonder if she had the chance to go back, would she make that phone call again? I don't even want to imagine what my life would be like if I hadn't met her.

When you come to a fork in the road, take it.

—YOGI BERRA
AMERICAN BASEBALL LEGEND

In the fall of 1998, a lot of major life events happened to me all at once. I passed the bar exam, got married, and immediately joined my father, where I cofounded my first company designing and building fountains. I had occasional thoughts of actually practicing law, but my plan had always been to join the family business. Unfortunately, around the same time my relationship with my dad and my stepmother began rapidly to deteriorate. Stacey comes from what I consider to be a relatively normal family, while I come from what I would classify as a high-functioning dysfunctional one. Maneuvering through minefields of guilt from all three of my parents felt normal to me when it was all I had known, but now being part of another family had opened my eyes. Constantly putting out all the little fires had become exhausting and frustrating, and I knew Stacey was completely out of her element. We planned to start our own family soon, which put an even greater emphasis on the type of environment in which we wanted our kids to grow up.

Family dynamics are often difficult to manage by themselves, but they can create untenable friction when intertwined with business. Because I had sacrificed professional independence, my career was a perpetual hostage to my personal state of affairs outside the office. In addition to that, I soon realized I wasn't happy or passionate about this business I had spent my life preparing for. Stacey had just become pregnant with our first child, Zach, and I began to seriously evaluate my life and consider making some big changes.

I had immense respect for Stacey's dad Carl, who owned a very successful packaging company based in Omaha. Stacey had been running his Chicago branch from our home, so I had become very familiar with the business. An opportunity became available for me to join Carl's company and start our family in Omaha. Everything in my life had swirled together at once, and after reflecting on it for a couple of months, I decided to make the change. My entire world was then in Chicago, and Stacey was actually reluctant to leave, but I needed some separation from my family and a healthier environment. In September of 2003,

I arrived in Omaha, Nebraska, without a single friend and our first baby due in a few months. We can all look back and point to one monumental decision that stands above all others in our lives. This was it for me.

I don't think my dad actually believed I was leaving until the day I drove away. I can still see him wiping his tears away as I left the office for the last time. I know he felt I had chosen Stacey's father over him, but I hope he respected my difficult decision to chart a new course. Moving was scary, but the Omaha community was unbelievably welcoming to us, and I made friends immediately. I found that I really enjoyed the packaging business and was fortunate to join an established and successful company. While it provided me with job security and a solid income, there was always an element of personal accomplishment missing for me. Soon thereafter, I truly learned the meaning of the saying "Be careful what you wish for." Less than four years after I got to Omaha, Carl made the decision to sell the company. Now I had to figure out what I was going to do, and it wouldn't be a smooth road.

Following the sale of the company, I did a number of different things with limited success. First, I traded options professionally, which required me to commute to Chicago during the week and travel home on the weekends. It was very difficult on Stacey and our young boys, Zach and Noah, who missed their dad. The most redeeming quality of this arrangement was that I stayed with my dad and stepmom while in Chicago; this arrangement greatly repaired our father-son bond. In addition, I made money trading, but it was clear that unless I lived near the action in Chicago, it wasn't going to work long-term. After a year, I moved back to Omaha full-time, got a real estate license and cofounded a property management company. I even dabbled in mobile app development.

After five years away from the industry, Carl "unretired" to join me in starting up a brand new packaging distribution company. A lot had changed in the interim, and we found ourselves fighting many of the same headwinds we used to create for other companies. I would eventually find those feelings of accomplishment I'd once craved, but not before experiencing several painful and costly lessons along the way.

I've learned a great deal along my life's journey of ups and downs. I've celebrated great successes and had to overcome devastating failures. I've made expensive professional and personal mistakes, which have affected me and those close to me. I've swung from feeling financially secure to genuinely worried about my ability to pay my bills. Through all the missteps and setbacks, I was always determined to make sense of it all, to learn, to grow, and ultimately to come out the other side stronger. I drew from the wisdom of others and gathered my own in the process.

Like many sons, I considered my dad as my role model when I was growing up. He was larger than life and he shared wisdom through anecdotes all the time. Through the years he had periodically written notes and letters to me, but that stopped when things became strained between us. I had convinced myself that he would never depart this world without having the last word with me, and I fully expected him to leave a road map behind full of explanations, advice, and regrets. That's the kind of person he was.

While I was on vacation in 2015, my stepmother called to let me know my dad had suffered a heart attack and was in a medically induced coma. I flew from California to Florida just in time to say good-bye without knowing if he actually heard me. After his death, I was crushed to learn there were no notes or letters left behind. Given all the wisdom he'd shared over the years, I found myself wondering why he hadn't packaged some of it into a final good-bye. Now, whatever I couldn't remember vanished with him. It was at that moment I thought of my kids, and how important it would be for me to take the collection of valuable lessons I've learned to date and memorialize it for them. I would put it in a book.

What I have discovered is that three things matter most in life: time, relationships, and money, in that order. They are our most precious assets and the goal of this book is to assist you in the ways you evaluate spending them. First and foremost is time, which is without question the most important asset for each of us. It is also the asset none of us can ever measure because we cannot know how much we have left. The time we do have is very much in our control, but we must choose how we spend it because we can never replace what is lost.

Next comes relationships—the people we choose to spend our time with. Life is a shared experience and the true measure of wealth is in the quality of our relationships. It begins with the relationship we have with ourselves. How well do we really understand ourselves, and how can we overcome our limitations? We'll examine how many of us create our own obstacles to work through. From there, our relationships extend out to our friends, spouses, and colleagues. We will see that it is the relationships we cultivate, as well as the relationships we separate ourselves from, that provide real meaning in our lives.

The last, and least important, of our three main assets, is money. I have spent a lot of time studying, and a little time working in, finance, so I will share some important lessons I've learned about making, growing, and spending money. The big takeaway, though, is that after our basic needs are met, more money isn't what provides us with more happiness. Money is not the panacea so many people waste their time and neglect their relationships in pursuit of.

As you read through the book, keep the following Venn diagram in your mind. Three different-sized circles: One for time, one for relationships, and one for money.

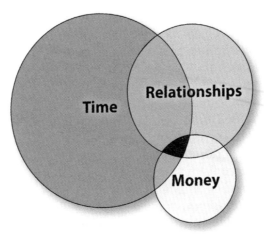

Everything meaningful in your life will fit into one of the three circles on the diagram. When you learn to use all of them wisely, you will find the most enriching experiences in the areas where they overlap. For example, time, relationships, and money all overlap when you take a vacation with those you love. Likewise, when you pay for a three-month course to improve your own knowledge or skill set. Both of these examples are likely to add lasting memories or value to your life.

Whenever I faced something challenging, my dad would remind me, "You know how you eat an elephant? One bite at a time." It's how I learned to approach any daunting task. It's how I recommend you approach the concepts in this book. Take a small bite here. Another bite there. Soon you will know the difference between creating meaningful change in your life and resigning yourself to accepting disappointment.

A great example of eating the elephant is Alabama football coach Nick Saban's famous "The Process." Coach Saban focuses on the little things. Blocking technique, precise route-running, and not jumping before the snap. He drills the "WIN" mentality into his players: *What's Important Now?* The Process is what has allowed Alabama to come from behind when they were losing. A huge deficit can feel like the weight of an elephant on you, and it can be discouraging. Saban teaches his players to ignore the scoreboard and focus only on the next play. If everyone does their job, and the play is successful, then do it again. Stay in the moment and trust The Process. Pretty soon the team has put a drive together and points on the board. Bite by bite, they get back into the game.

There is no substitute for a life lived and there is no better teacher than experience. However, along my journey I have found universal truths that are surprisingly common to all of us. My hope is that this book will provide the wisdom for you to make better decisions, get more out of your life, and give yourself a higher percentage shot at your dreams.

Part I

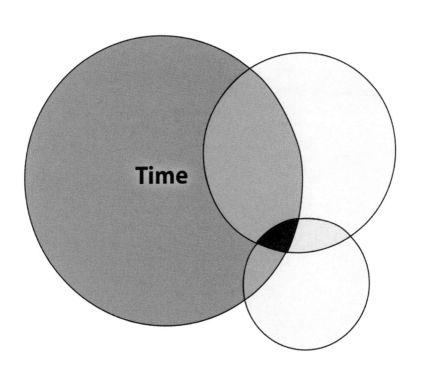

1

Time Is Irreplaceable

Time is a strange thing. As our lives go by, it
means absolutely nothing. And then, one fine day,
we are aware of nothing else.

—RICHARD STRAUSS,
GERMAN COMPOSER

The one thing you will never be able to replace
is time. More money can be earned. Homes
can be rebuilt. Possessions will always come and go, and
many weren't necessary in the first place. Time is our
single most valuable asset and yet it is the one we cannot
measure. All we can do is choose how to spend what we
have remaining. Sadly, as our time rolls by, we too often
waste it being overcome with negative emotions about
our past or our future. Meanwhile, one is gone forever,
and the other is uncertain. What you're about to learn is
the importance of right now—the moments you actually
live in.

Before reading Carlo Rovelli's *The Order of Time,* I
was fairly confident I understood exactly what time was.
Rovelli is a brilliant quantum physicist who challenged
the limits of my imagination. He argues that the past
and the future do not actually exist, that time moves at
different speeds depending on your location, and that we

are not actually things but processes. But Rovelli is also a philosopher, and the most compelling and enjoyable sections of the book are those in which he suggests that time is life, that humans are "beings made of time." When it is gone, we are no more. It reinforced for me just how vital the concept of time is to the quality of our lives.

Youth was wonderful.
What a pity it had to be wasted on the young!

—GEORGE BERNARD SHAW,
IRISH PLAYWRIGHT

Of course, we never truly appreciate being young until we are older. From the first day we open our eyes, our identity is being somebody's child. Through the years we go—toddlers to teenagers. Our little world expands until one day we wake up in our own bed in our own home planning our own future. A stark realization hits us: We're not somebody's child anymore. We've become adults.

Remember how you couldn't wait to sit at the grown-ups' table? Remember how you couldn't wait to graduate? Remember how you couldn't wait to move out of the house and make your own rules? Remember how you couldn't wait to be done with school and work for a living? Remember how you couldn't wait to start a family of your own? One day, without even realizing it, you stepped through the portal into a new dimension. All your life, everything you wanted was off in the future. Now, you begin yearning to go back in time.

With a final tip of the cap to Rovelli, I have often felt time does, in fact, alter its speed. The next birthday always seems to show up faster than the last one did. Time flies when you're having fun, and it slows to a crawl when you're stuck at an unnecessary meeting or function. Yet, regardless at what speed the time moves, it's still gone.

It's gone after you've binge-watched a show on Netflix. It's gone after you've scrolled through years of someone else's vacation photos on social media. Just think about all the times you've thought to yourself, "That's two hours of my life I'll never get back."

The same people who say "Time is money" would never toss $500 into the wind but they give no second thoughts to spending countless days on trivial activities. They won't waste their money, but they willingly waste their time. You can get only one of those back. Focusing on what is really important to us and developing good habits to stay on track is how we consistently generate real meaning in our lives.

2

Habits

People do not decide their futures.
They decide their habits
and their habits decide their futures.

—F.M. ALEXANDER,
AUSTRALIAN AUTHOR

Human beings are creatures of habit and, though we like to believe that we are actively making our own choices in the world, 90 percent of what most of us do on a given day follows a routine. Our routines consist of many habits we have developed, and they are difficult to change. When we have ingrained a series of bad habits, we are putting our time-wasting efforts on autopilot. The reverse is also true. Productive habits make far better use of our time.

Wisdom is available to all of us when we are receptive, but simply hearing a good idea isn't enough to automatically change our behavior. We have to commit to acting on it. As James Clear points out in *Atomic Habits*, we often "leave it up to chance and hope we will 'just remember to do it' or feel motivated at the right time. An implementation intention sweeps away foggy notions like 'I want to work out more,' 'I want to be more productive,' or 'I should vote,' and transforms them into a concrete plan of action." It begins by saying 'I will work out for twenty minutes every morning,' 'Here are the ways I will be more productive,' and 'I will vote on Tuesday morning.' Making a commitment ensures you will do it. Do it enough, and it becomes a habit.

Where is the wisdom we have lost in knowledge?
Where is the knowledge we have lost in
information?

—T.S. ELIOT,
AMERICAN-ENGLISH POET

One of my college friends is now a successful businessman who has been passionate about self-improvement. Nearly every month, he would recommend a new self-help or business book to me. At the rate he was reading them, I could not imagine him having the time to effectively implement all the new concepts he was learning. All this reading is like drinking from a fire hose. Gushes of information miss the mark. "That's why the philosophers warn us not to be satisfied with mere learning, but to add practice and then training," the ancient Greek Stoic Epictetus said, "for as time passes, we forget what we learned."

You can't help but absorb new ideas and insights by reading more, but learning about something and integrating it are not the same thing. I recommended my friend read *Atomic Habits*, or *The Power of Habit* by Charles Duhigg, to understand the opportunities he was missing. To make any good idea stick, it has to become a habit first.

Knowledge and experience work together. Books reveal the secrets to life, but many of the potential benefits fade in time if they aren't implemented. The brain simply cannot retain everything, and over time new inputs displace older inputs that weren't imprinted. There is a key distinction between understanding something and internalizing it. For example, I understood "The Road Not Taken" by Robert Frost, but I internalized "The Gambler" by Kenny Rogers. While I read Frost's poem once, my dad played "The Gambler" over and over in his car. Both contain invaluable life lessons, but the repetition of hearing the song kept it fresh in my mind.

Think of it another way: When you slap something on quickly with adhesive, it will stick for a short while. But when you take the time to weave it into the fabric, it will hold a lot longer. Wisdom comes not from adding new knowledge and information, but rather from truly integrating its meaning and context.

Albert Einstein said, "Paper is to write things down that we need to remember. Our brains are used to think." A good habit I recommend everyone develop is writing in a journal. They aren't just for songwriters and poets. Tim Ferriss's *Tools of Titans* reveals just how many successful entrepreneurs and innovators swear by them. Marcus Aurelius, the most powerful man in the Roman Empire, kept a journal, which was eventually published as the book *Meditations*.

Likewise, many of the sections in this book were pulled from my own notebooks. Use your journal to record your ideas, evaluate and manage your priorities, memorialize meaningful conversations, and record important concepts from the book you are reading. If you'd prefer keeping your notes in an app on a tablet, that's fine, too. Whatever tool you employ, the value of maintaining a written record for you to reflect upon at the beginning and ending of each day, each month, and each year cannot be overstated. Your journal is your own fountain of wisdom and you should visit it often.

When we repeat things consistently, they become habits. That is why so many golfers spend hours practicing their swing. Never confuse activity with achievement, however. Consider that about 65 percent of all golf shots take place within 100 yards of the pin. That means in an eighteen-hole round we will take only about fourteen swings with our driver. With that level of discrepancy, we know that the biggest impact would come from improving our chipping and putting. Instead, we spend most of our practice time blasting away on the driving range. We may develop a consistently long and straight drive through practice repetitions, but it may come at the expense of the most important part of the game.

Anything we do consistently will become a habit, and this applies to both good and bad behaviors. In order to guide our habits, we need to set and maintain our priorities. Priorities are what keep us focused on making the most out of our time.

3

Priorities

*First tell yourself what kind of person you want to
be, then do what you have to do.*

—Epictetus,
Greek philosopher

Not only is time always moving but it will
consistently expand to fill the empty spaces
you leave for it. Time isn't going to blow a whistle on
itself and tell you to get back on track; it will continue
stretching as far as you allow it to. Business meetings
are a perfect example. A skillful manager is able to hold
a productive meeting in thirty to sixty minutes. Yet, far
too often these same meetings are scheduled for up to
three times longer and never finish early. More often than
not, the root cause is a fundamental lack of respect for
others' time. After all, we can always find something to
discuss when there is a captive audience. Unfortunately,
your ability to force this type of change at work may be
limited. Outside the workplace, however, it is completely
within your control to develop greater respect for your
own time.

Some people take life as it comes, drifting from
one interaction to the next, enjoying the randomness of

the journey. Others schedule rigidly, leaving very little room for variation in their lives. I find myself happiest somewhere in the middle. I focus intently on the things that are most important to me, and one of those things is the joy of occasional spontaneity. My friend Scott has always said, "The best times in life are unplanned," and I have found that to be true. Some of my favorite memories began as spur-of-the-moment decisions. Road trips. Backyard Wiffle ball games. Fishing until sunset. These and other meaningful events only happened because I intentionally left enough room in my life for flexibility. Ironically, by not overloading your time with wasteful activities, you are actually scheduling pockets of emptiness that can be filled when the most special opportunities come along. It demonstrates one of my favorite equations: addition by subtraction. We increase the value of something simply by removing that which is wasteful. Addition by subtraction can, and should, be applied to *time, relationships, and money.*

Time management begins with a clear understanding of your priorities. Your priorities guide you. They are your compass. They are the things that matter most. Most importantly, they are *limited in scope.* One of the biggest mistakes people make is thinking they can accomplish too many things at once. As New England Patriots coach Bill Belichick told a rookie quarterback named Tom Brady, "You're trying to see everything and instead you're seeing nothing." Business consultant John Ninkovich has a similar philosophy: "If everything is a priority, then nothing is a priority."

Having a clear understanding of your key priorities will help you navigate through the minefield of time wasters you'll be faced with every day. Phone calls, e-mails, social media, Web browsing, television…and the list goes on and on. Successfully addressing your priorities will give you peace of mind, a sense of accomplishment, and an improved level of happiness. Failing to identify your priorities, or allowing yourself to be distracted from them, will cause you to feel overwhelmed, generate feelings of failure, and elevate your overall stress level.

Priorities exist on multiple planes. The most effective way to set priorities is by using a top-down approach, beginning with your high-level priorities. These are the most important things you want in life right now. Intermediate priorities are the major goals along the way that will help you get there. Finally, short-term priorities are the tasks required to reach those intermediate goals that are generally completed within a day or two. Consider your life as a road trip. Your high-level priorities are your GPS system. They guide you toward your destination, who you want to be, and what you want to accomplish. Your intermediate priorities are the big cities you pass along the way. They are the significant milestones you aim for, and they mark your progress on your journey. Finally, your short-term priorities are all the little things you do (as well as the little things you *don't* do) between the mile markers. Time is your tank of gas. When all your priorities are aligned, you are zooming down the road with maximum efficiency.

High-Level Priorities

Your college team winning a basketball game against a rival is a big victory. Winning the conference championship is a huge victory. But winning the National Championship is a *monumental* victory. Think of your high-level priorities as the monumental victories you are aiming for in your life. They are the major achievements and the ones you will be most proud of if you succeed. Working toward a high-level priority requires serious commitment and a major investment in time. We set our high-level priorities first, and then cascade them down to our intermediate and short-term priorities. All three must be in alignment.

High-level priorities will vary by person and change naturally as our lives evolve. The arc of Tom Brady's football career exemplifies this. Heading into his senior year at Michigan, Brady's high-level priority was remaining the team's starting quarterback. In fact, Brady ended up sharing quarterback duties with Drew Henson his final college season. As for dreams of playing in the NFL, Brady wasn't sure he was going to get drafted at all. Heading into the 2000 NFL draft, the scouting report on Brady was that he "looked slow" and "was not impressive." At the time of the draft, Brady had literally been putting his resume together for a potential career in finance.

Seven teams drafted quarterbacks before the New England Patriots finally selected Tom Brady in the sixth round. The team intended for him to be a potential backup to franchise quarterback Drew Bledsoe. Coach Belichick, who didn't even call Brady after the draft, said, "We'll just put him out there with everybody else and let him compete and we'll see what happens." Brady's new high-level priority became making the team and being good enough to stay there. "I'm really trying to stay out there and take a lot of the mental reps, and I see what Drew does out there," he said at the time.

Brady beat out the other two backups to Bledsoe. Then, in the second game of Brady's second season with the team, Bledsoe suffered a severe injury. Few fans expected Brady to succeed at all, but he had mastered the ability of focusing on—and adjusting—his high-level priorities as his career evolved. Brady no longer saw himself as the backup; his new high-level priority was to remain the team's starting quarterback. After Brady led the Patriots to their first Super Bowl win that season, Bledsoe was never able to regain his starting job.

It's safe to say Tom Brady succeeded, winning three league MVP awards, six Super Bowl championships, and four Super Bowl MVP awards with the Patriots. Brady could have retired a Patriot at forty-two years old with nothing more to prove. However, in 2020, he set a new high-level priority when he left the Patriots for the Tampa Bay Buccaneers, a team that hadn't won a single play-off game in sixteen years. Even after proving critics wrong while becoming arguably the greatest quarterback of all time, Brady was doubted once again. And guess what? He still led the Bucs to an improbable and incredible Super Bowl win in his first year with the team!

Your high-level priorities are what bring real meaning to your life. Some are personal: raising children, owning a home, developing a hobby, or traveling to places around the world. Some are professional: being promoted, making partner, starting your own business, or finding a more meaningful line of work. You're never too young to begin setting meaningful high-level priorities either. When my oldest son, Zach, was eleven years old, he was intensely focused on eventually making the high school baseball team. That goal meant everything to him and drove his hard work and training through years of competitive baseball.

Like Tom Brady, Zach didn't pay a lot of attention to the people who told him he didn't have a chance. Not only did Zach make the freshmen baseball team and have a productive season, he immediately set his sights on making junior varsity. When we achieve one high-level priority, it becomes a new starting point for our next one.

High-level priorities can also embody philosophies rather than achievements. In other words, the way you get to the finish line can be even more important than reaching it. A member of the clergy, for example, would consider living by a set of principles to be a high-level priority. As such, intermediate and short-term priorities should remain connected to these principles. In 1973, two Princeton social psychologists, John Darley and Daniel Batson, set up an experiment to see how easily this connection could be broken.

Darley and Batson arranged for a group of seminary students to first complete questionnaires about their own religion in one building. The students were then sent to a second building to give a talk about the Good Samaritan, a famous parable about the only person who stopped to help a bleeding man in the road. Some of the students were told to hurry to the next building because they were running late for their talk. The researchers had cleverly planted a man slumped over in an alleyway, in obvious need of help, directly in the path of the seminary students.

It might seem shocking to consider that even after being primed by questions about their religion, and despite heading over to give a talk about the Good Samaritan, some students literally stepped over the man in distress on their way to the next building! The religious students had allowed a short-term diversion (being late) to completely override their high-level priority (living virtuously), even though it was fresh in their minds. You might say these students certainly weren't practicing what they were hurrying over to preach!

What the Princeton experiment shows is that even people who want to be closer to God can lose their way from time to time. We are all guilty of it at one time or another. I recently experienced it myself when I planned a summer road trip for my sons, Zach and Noah. One of my highest priorities is spending as much quality time as possible with my kids while they are still living at home. I want to create as many special memories as I can for them to look back on when they're older. What could possibly derail a fun trip with my boys? Spoiler alert: It was me.

I had the entire first day planned out, beginning with the time we would be leaving the house. When it was time to go, Zach wasn't ready, and Noah hadn't eaten breakfast yet. I immediately chastised them for mismanaging their time and, following a delayed departure, I made a quick stop to grab breakfast for Noah. A slow cashier and an indecisive customer ahead of me continued to pile on the minutes. Shaking my head, I opened the car door to find the boys laughing hysterically. "What could possibly be funny right now?" I asked them. "Noah forgot his EpiPen at home," Zach said with a smile from ear to ear. This time I really laid into them and the laughter stopped.

By the time we got on the road, we were only forty-five minutes late. In my anger, I completely lost sight of the big picture: the time we were supposed to enjoy being together. For a relatively minor delay out of a seven-hour drive, I created a memory for them all right. Just not the one they were supposed to remember. What I should have done is laugh off every setback along with the boys and make it a group joke. But just like those seminary students, I lost sight of my high-level priority and ended up sabotaging my own interests. It's going to happen to all of us, and it's not fatal. We just have to figure it out and get back on track. We may or may not get another opportunity to do better next time, but we definitely will never have that time back.

Whatever your own individual goals might look like, the key question to answer is, "What outcomes will bring the most happiness in my life?" These are your high-level priorities. Once you've identified them, be sure you keep them in mind and always pull yourself back when you begin to drift away. Remember, that's what your GPS system is for.

Action Exercise

Identify your high-level priorities as they exist today. Here is the perfect opportunity to write in your journal.

What are the things that get you excited? Is it success at work? What is that next big milestone? Are you in line for a promotion or partnership? Is it school-related? Is it graduating or attaining a license? Maybe you want to create something of your own. Is it family-related? A trip with your spouse or doing something with your kids? If you can list more than three high-level priorities, you should consider narrowing it down.

What will it mean to you if you can accomplish them? Are these the most important goals for you right now? Why are they so important? Are they worth the time investment you will have to make to get there?

Intermediate Priorities and Accountability

Intermediate priorities are the larger projects and commitments that fit within your high-level priorities. For a young person, making a team or a performance group, achieving academic excellence, and developing different skills are some examples of intermediate priorities. For adults, some examples might include business projects, coaching, volunteer work, or vacation planning. Regardless of what commitments you identify to attain your high-level priorities, you are going to have to make time sacrifices in order to accomplish them.

If becoming an attorney is my high-level priority, there are some major steps along the way I will have to complete in order to get there. I know I first have to graduate from college and take the LSAT exam—a requirement for law school admission. And, unless I'm truly fortunate, I need to save or borrow money to pay for law school. Those would be intermediate priorities. If my high-level priority is to make a business or career change, then I know I have to update my resume, meet with headhunters, and network with colleagues who can help me. I might have to write a business plan and meet with investors. Those would be my intermediate priorities.

15

If my high-level priority is to take a special vacation, then my intermediate priorities would include saving money, researching travel options, and making reservations.

These things aren't going to happen by themselves just because we want them to. Unfortunately, we are far better at identifying and discussing opportunities than we are at committing to and executing them. With the constant bombardment of distractions increasing daily, we have to intentionally set aside the time to focus on the few most important things. Creating accountability is the key to accomplishing any goal we set. As executive coach and author Marshall Goldsmith explains, "most of us understand, we just don't do." When we don't establish the expectation of precisely *when* the task will be completed, it becomes "something we will get to later."

If we want to reasonably hold someone, including ourselves, accountable, then we need to set clear expectations. For example, "Is it reasonable for me to expect you to have this completed by Friday afternoon?" is a specific task with a set deadline. "I will write a chapter of this book each month" is a specific task with a defined time frame. Conversely, "I have to take a closer look at our expenses" or "I really need to lose some weight" are both nonspecific tasks with open-ended completion dates. The odds are against those two things getting done.

I have managed many salespeople myself and worked with different sales managers throughout my career. Every one of them, including me, credits their own particular management style as the reason for their success. After all, were they not selected for that role rather than someone else? I have been lucky to work alongside another sales manager, Ken, whom I truly enjoy and consider a friend outside the workplace. Each of us manages a different group of salespeople for half the country.

Ken and I agree on many things, but we have different management philosophies. He believes strongly in the value of data, placing a high importance on computer entry and reporting. I believe strongly in understanding what each salesperson feels they need in order to be most productive, and I try to be as flexible as I can with the tools used. The most important data to me has always been the results. I'm still not sure which of us is right or wrong, and it ultimately doesn't matter much. Despite our different styles and philosophies, we have both been successful. Why? Because we both establish clear expectations for our salespeople and manage to those expectations. We develop individual budgets and we hold our folks accountable to them each and every month. If you don't have that cornerstone in place, it doesn't matter how fancy your computer programs are.

Without establishing accountability, we put ourselves at risk of indulging our natural human propensity to procrastinate. If we know our tasks aren't expected in the near future, they will default to low urgency and be set aside. This is precisely where our priority-setting process will save us. By making something a priority, we will be less likely to put it off, regardless of how much time we have to complete it. For example: If you've made a work promotion a high-level priority, then shining at your year-end review would certainly be an intermediate priority. Add to that the potential incentive of a year-end bonus or a raise, and you are less likely to leave an important work project hanging out there, regardless of how much time you have to complete it.

Without developing the discipline to organize our priorities and systematically attack them, we will float from one thing to the next like a boat on a lake without reaching the other side. To prevent us from drifting further from our goals, our intermediate priorities become the oars that steer us back on course.

Action Exercise

Take a look at the high-level priorities you set earlier. Now identify two or three intermediate priorities that fit within those high-level priorities.

Are there projects or assignments due in the future?

Are there contracts or other documents you need to have prepared or executed?

Are there personal financial milestones you need to meet?

Are there meetings you need to set?

Once you've identified those milestones that move you toward your high-level priorities, set a deadline for each one by which it must be completed.

Short-Term Priorities

Priorities cascade down from the top. First, we identify our high-level priorities, which are the most meaningful goals in our lives at the moment. From there, we identify our intermediate priorities which all fit neatly within those high-level goals. Now it's time to zero in on our short-term priorities. These are our daily activities, the ones most susceptible to disruption. Remember our metaphorical road trip from earlier? High-level priorities are the GPS system, intermediate priorities are the big cities along the way and short-term priorities are all the things you do between the mile markers.

Here is a real-life example of how short-term priorities are defined and addressed. A few years ago, I was in the backseat of my father's car as he drove around and around a cemetery searching for my grandfather's grave. We had a paper map and still could not find our way. I fired off a sarcastic text message to my friend Scott telling him, "You need to invent a mobile app that lets you mark gravestones and find them again, so I never have to get dizzy driving around like this again." That joke was the start of RestingSpot, our company that would attempt to map the world's cemeteries using crowdsourcing and GPS.

Without getting too far into the business plan, our high-level priorities were to:

- Launch a user-friendly GPS-based mobile app that enables people to mark gravesites themselves, and then guide anyone to their locations via their smartphones.

- Maintain an attractive and well-designed Website that aggregates and integrates that GPS data, and also allows for additional add-ins like messaging, memorials, and floral deliveries.

These were two straightforward high-level priorities. Next, our intermediate priorities were to:

- Have a proposed design layout for an app and Website ready to present to our design contractors in two weeks' time.

- Work with design contractors to have a functional app and Website ready for initial field testing in two months' time.

- Have the app and Website ready for launch within six months' time.

From the top-down, we first define our high-level priorities and then set the intermediate priorities and timelines to reach them. After those clear goals and deadlines have been set, it is our short-term priorities that will get us there little by little, bite by bite.

Our very first RestingSpot milestone was having layouts for the Website and mobile app ready to present to our designers in two weeks. This required us to define a key short-term priority as gathering ideas we liked from existing platforms and translating those to a written flow-chart. We compared notes for an hour each evening and synchronized our ideas. Like most people, Scott and I also had the usual work and family obligations that greatly limited our available free time. This forced us to grab whatever available opportunities we could find during the day. Focusing on our goals and timelines made it far easier to eliminate distractions and other diversions that might have otherwise interfered with our short-term priorities.

Once our designers delivered our beta Website and mobile app, we had a four-month timeline to meet our high-priority goal of an official launch. Our intermediate priorities involved perfecting different sections of the platform. Our short-term priorities involved finding time each day to visit a cemetery, mark some graves, and take detailed notes on functionality and suggested tweaks. Working with a technology design company based in India had its benefits. In addition to a manageable cost structure, the time difference enabled us to present our daily findings during videoconference meetings late at night, go to sleep, and then wake up to fresh updates already implemented.

This project would have been overwhelming if we hadn't structured our priorities the way we had. With a clear vision of what needed to be accomplished each day, we were able to set aside television shows, social media distractions and other non-essential activities and focus on what was meaningful to us. In the end, we were able to meet our goals and we did launch a mobile app and a Website.

RestingSpot ultimately turned out to be a better idea than a business, but our success in developing it illustrates the importance of linking our priorities together. Once we've set our priorities from the top down, we begin to work them from the bottom up. The short-term priorities we address during our days allow us to reach our intermediate priorities, which in turn get us closer to achieving our high-level priorities.

E-mails, meetings, groceries, exercise, cleaning, organizing, homework, and carpools are some of the many tasks each of us have. Unfortunately, we also face

---

Action Exercise

Each morning, make a list of your short-term priorities. Do they align with your intermediate priorities? Look over the intermediate priorities you set.

Are there bites you can take out of those work projects?

Are there customers you need to call? Is there any reading or research you need to do?

Is there something you need to help your spouse or kids with?

Are there appointments or plans to make?

At the end of each day, review the list and grade yourself. How well did you address your short-term priorities today?

---

an unrelenting barrage of distractions that can easily push us off course. There is nothing wrong with mindless entertainment when we've got a few minutes to unwind. We all deserve to reward ourselves by relaxing a bit after a long day, a stressful project, or a busy week. Just remember, television shows can wait for us to watch them. Social media won't shut down if we don't check in. Focus on your priorities, and your priorities will keep you focused on what you need to do to be productive at any given moment.

The people who fail to put together a game plan end up wandering through their days, putting out fires, and dealing primarily with whatever is right in front of them. In this purely *reactive* mode, the meaningful is inadvertently neglected in favor of the meaningless. Only by being *proactive* will we be able to accomplish our goals and make the most of our time. Our short-term priorities are the checklist that keeps us on track. We identify those necessary responsibilities for ourselves early in the day, and then hold ourselves accountable to them before we say goodnight.

Be honest and critical. "I ended up arguing with someone on Facebook so I didn't get to finish the report," is one example. "I knocked everything out early and was able to go to the beach" is another. Grading yourself keeps you accountable. These little wins and losses will begin to strengthen your mind and drive lasting change in your life.

Priorities in Action: Putting the System to Work

Setting top-down priorities is the way we make seemingly impossible tasks possible. Consider the following exchange between Team USA hockey coaches Herb Brooks and Lou Nanne as they discuss taking on the invincible Soviets in the film *Miracle:*

> **Herb:** My goal is to beat 'em at their own game.
>
> **Lou:** Beat the best team in the world? Gold medalists in '64, '68, '72, '76? Pretty lofty goal, Herb.
>
> **Herb:** Well, Lou, that's why I want to pursue it.

The book in your hands was a pretty lofty goal, too. If you want a tangible success of this priority-setting system, you're reading it. I had never attempted something of this magnitude before. Although many of the articles I have written required research and idea development, those were only a handful of pages. I have also edited full-length books, but that content had already been created by others. The idea of writing this entire book, including conceptualizing, organizing, and editing, was a daunting one to say the least.

Even though I had been compiling many topics, ideas, and notes, I wasn't convinced I'd be able to generate enough meaningful material, or that anyone would actually buy it if I did. To top it off, I had also been warned by an author friend that my odds of actually having a book published were miniscule, and I might be wasting my time. Solid pep talk, Fred!

I had reached the point at which all of us are most vulnerable to being overwhelmed by self-doubt, scared away from a dream, prepared to accept that we just aren't meant to do certain things. When you find yourself face-to-face with the elephant, it's decision time. You either shrink from the challenge and walk away, or you grab your knife and fork and get to work. Remember this: If you don't feel doubt and uncertainty, if you aren't more than a little uncomfortable, then you probably haven't set your goal high enough. I committed to make this book a high-level priority. I still wasn't entirely certain whether or not I was capable of pulling it off, but I was certain something silly like fear wouldn't prevent me from trying.

I used to think people who talked to themselves in the mirror were crazy. Then, one day, I decided to test it out myself. Every morning I looked into my own eyes and said, "I am happy and grateful for what I have" out loud. At first, I felt like Stuart Smalley from *Saturday Night Live,* but over a period of days and weeks I gradually noticed that I actually did feel happier overall, and I was actually enjoying the people in my life more. This is the incredible power of making declarations; unfortunately, people refuse to do it because it seems corny. While you can't just say the magic words and expect a miracle to happen, my experiment proved to me that, by incorporating this daily habit, you can absolutely steer your mind on a different course. Which is helpful information given that every achievement in our lives begins with the right mind-set.

Declarations are tailor-made for high-level priorities. Hearing your own voice stating what you are going to accomplish provides surprisingly powerful motivation. "I'm going to do this" is a call to arms for your confidence and a stern rebuke to your fears. Not only did I say "I'm going to write a book" to myself out loud, but I also made it a point to say those words to my wife. Now I had doubled my accountability. Note that I didn't say "I'm going to become an author." If that were my high-level priority, then writing this book would be an intermediate-term priority, along with other books I would eventually write. At the moment, becoming an author would introduce additional variables and concerns with respect to my current career, my family, and the hobbies I enjoy participating in. Be clear about your intentions.

One thing I did not expect was for my declaration to generate any negative feelings or anxiety in my wife, but that is exactly what it did. For some time now, Stacey has been developing a very interesting idea for a television series in her head. Despite her clear passion for this project, she believes only a "professional" screenwriter is capable or suitable to bring her vision to life. The creator of the television series *Mad Men*, Matthew Weiner, would disagree with her. "Actually write the script," he said, "There's no arguing with an existing piece of material, and you don't have to rely on anyone else's imagination." After all, who is in a better position to bring our own ideas to reality than ourselves?

Rather than throwing her ideas down on paper to see what happens, Stacey only sees an elephant in her way. I hope that seeing me work on this book will inspire her to ignore those artificial barriers and get started. To turn your ideas into something real, you have to turn them into priorities first.

---

*The journey of a thousand miles
begins with a single step.*

—LAO TZU,
CHINESE PHILOSOPHER

I had my road map laid out. My high-level priority was completing this book within a year's time. The intermediate priorities were organizing and completing the major sections and chapters of the book at set intervals. The more I penciled out the general structure and overview, the more my confidence began to snowball. This once-daunting project now had a visible path to completion, and I could identify the individual tasks I needed to accomplish in order to get there. The only remaining challenges to bringing this dream to reality were my short-term priorities. I needed to isolate pockets of time in my schedule where none seemingly existed before. I committed to find a way to clear out time slots for writing, and then attack this thing bit by bit and chapter by chapter. I just never expected it to be so difficult.

Short-Term Struggles: Fighting for Focus

What I do today is very important because I am exchanging a day of my life for it.

—HEARTSILL WILSON,
AMERICAN AUTOMOTIVE EXECUTIVE
AND MOTIVATIONAL SPEAKER

To hit my milestones and finish this book within a year, I would have to make progress consistently every week. My biggest challenge would be finding and allocating enough free space during my days to think, compose, and edit. Writing requires maintaining discipline and focus for long periods of time in order to truly capture what you are trying to say. In his landmark book, *Flow: The Psychology of Optimum Experience,* Mihaly Csikszentmihalyi explores the experience of "flow," which is the mental state most conducive to productivity. I needed to tap into that.

Unfortunately, like most adults, I don't have the luxury of completely setting aside my business responsibilities during the workday. It doesn't get much easier in the evenings either. With a wife and young children, truly "free" time is difficult to come by and even more difficult to sacrifice. Unless everyone was already occupied (a rare occurrence), I refused to neglect prime family time by isolating myself during the evening hours. That left early mornings as my only reliable option for consistent writing.

Not all readers are leaders,
but all leaders are readers.

—HARRY S. TRUMAN,
THIRTY-THIRD PRESIDENT
OF THE UNITED STATES

When I was eight years old, my grandfather gave me advice that had an enormous impact on the rest of my life. He said, "I don't care what it is, but you need to choose *something* to read every day." I've never forgotten those words, and I've been reading books every day since. I'll read any nonfiction book that looks interesting to me, and I mix it up by sprinkling in a handful of novels.

I've maintained the same routine for years: Every morning, I wake up when everyone else is asleep, pour a cup of coffee, and read as long as possible. Those early quiet hours have become a form of meditation for me whether I'm home or out of town. I also feel that when I start the day learning something new, I've primed myself to continue learning when I leave the house. It's been a daily priority for longer than I can remember. Sadly, I had to accept the reality that this valued part of my day would have to be temporarily repurposed if I was ever going to complete my own book and not cause a major disruption to my life.

I began devoting my entire mornings to writing. Almost immediately I began feeling different during the days, and it was starting to affect me. It was a psychological withdrawal syndrome, like something was missing. In the past, I had been able to set everything else aside and focus intensely for bursts of time to write a blog post or work on a business plan, but not for any great length of time. I knew this arrangement would not be sustainable, and if I didn't change the plan I would never stick with it.

My solution was to divide my mornings into address-ing both priorities: one half reading and the other half writing. While it would undoubtedly extend my comple-tion date, it was an acceptable compromise to bring a much-needed balance back into my life. A willingness to be flexible allows you to stay in the game, continue taking small bites of the elephant, and not overwhelm yourself into failure.

Doubt and fear are powerful negative influences that will find you and cling to you if you let them. I faced both, and we will deal with those in greater detail shortly. For now, I want to address a different mental roadblock: the rising opportunity costs. This is a concept many people ignore, but it is very real, and something to keep front and center in your mind. Essentially, whenever you choose something in your life, you lose the benefit of every other alternative you could have chosen instead. Those lost benefits are called the *opportunity costs*. This concept is often associated with money spent or invested.

For example, if you spent $3,000 on a trip, rather than investing it in the stock market, your opportunity cost is whatever stock gains you missed out on. Opportunity costs are higher to us when applied to time, our most precious asset. Every minute we choose to spend on one thing is another minute taken away from something else. As our time commitment for one thing grows, the opportunity costs for everything else grow as well.

The more time I devoted to this book, the more I risked losing if it doesn't work out. This concern hung over me during the entire writing process. I questioned myself again and again. What have I lost if I spend all this time and effort and never finish it? What if I do finish it, and nobody is interested? Thanks to the inspiration I drew from the many successful people I read about every morning, I remained determined to stay the course. I learned how every famous person had to face down their own fears and insecurities at some point. Before the world knew their names, they had asked themselves the same questions I was asking myself. I realized in my heart that I would be able to live with all the time spent working on this book. But I would never be able to live with the regret of not giving it my best shot.

Twenty years from now you will be more disappointed by the things that you didn't do than by the ones you did do.

—MARK TWAIN,
AMERICAN AUTHOR
AND HUMORIST

In *Emotional Equations,* entrepreneur and author Chip Conley identified the two saddest words in the English language as "if only." "If only" refers to the things we could have done but didn't. Conley shares the eye-opening insights from a series of surveys that clearly reveal that people later regret "failures to act" twice as much as "regrettable actions." The takeaway: Whenever we don't act on something now, we create a potentially distressing "if only" moment for later.

The two things most likely to prevent us from acting now are experience and fear. We have the actual experiences from every time we've said something horribly wrong or made a silly mistake to look back on. We know how it turned out, we know how it made us feel, and we can call up that memory for help. We can tell ourselves, "Oh no, I'm not doing that again!" That's the benefit of learning from experience. However, when we are faced with a totally new and unfamiliar situation, seeking our memories only provides fragmented guidance. Moving forward is a risk, and risks can feel threatening. That creates the fear, and it is often a terribly misguided emotion.

The decision to give up is often a lot easier to accept today than it will be later on. Before you let go of something potentially meaningful, you'd better understand the reasons why. You'd also better understand that uncertainly looking forward is a lot less painful than uncertainty looking backward. Imagine yourself nearing the end of your years and reflecting back on your life. What are those big things you really wanted to do but never did? Will you still be wondering then how it might have turned out if only you'd decided to give it a shot today? What did you trade away your opportunity for? Was it really worth it?

In his autobiography, musician Jeff Tweedy wrote this moving passage about making the most of our time:

> No one has ever laid on their deathbed thinking, "Thank god I didn't make that song. Thank god I didn't make that piece of art. Thank god I avoided the embarrassment of putting a bad poem into the world." Nobody reaches the end of their life and regrets even a single moment of creating something, no matter how shitty or unappreciated that something might have been. I'm writing this just weeks after returning from Belleville, where I sat next to my dad's bed in my childhood house and watched him die. I can guarantee you that in the final moments of his life, he wasn't kicking himself for all those times when he dared to make a fool of himself by singing too loud.

When we reach the point in our lives at which we have more time behind us than ahead of us, we begin to more strongly contemplate the decisions we've made over the years. "Older people who have tried to achieve their dreams are always happier with their lives," Marshall Goldsmith writes, "So the key question is not, 'Did I make all my dreams come true?' The key question is, 'Did I try?'"

Action Exercise

Think about your big dreams, the "maybe in another life" kind.

Is there a place you want to visit?

Is there a city you want to live in?

Is there a career you think you have a real talent for?

Is there something artistic you want to create?

Is there someone you're afraid to ask out on a date?

Whatever those truly meaningful things are that get you excited but seem unlikely to happen, write them down. Keep them close to you. Picture yourself at the end of your life and looking back on the things you decided not to do. Try making one of them a high priority now and see if you can lay out a plan to make it happen. You know, just for fun.

Time is a zero-sum game, which is why everything we do carries an opportunity cost along with it. Whenever we choose one thing, another has to lose out. This becomes increasingly more difficult as the sacrifices grow in importance to us. Forfeiting video games or Web browsing generates far less internal friction than telling our kids we don't have time to play catch right now. We must always give serious thought to our priorities and constantly evaluate whether they are aligned with our sense of purpose and happiness. If they aren't, then it's definitely time to make some immediate adjustments.

A Final Word on Setting Priorities

The legendary golfer Jack Nicklaus said that 80 percent of a successful golf shot begins with properly gripping the club and the way you stand over the ball. In other words, before you've even moved a muscle, the majority of the work for success or failure has already been completed. Setting up your priorities, from the top all the way down, employs the same philosophy. Set up your shots properly, and you'll find the greens in life more than the sand traps.

4

Three Components of Time

You will never find time for anything.
If you want time, you must make it.

—CHARLES BUXTON,
ENGLISH BREWER, WRITER,
AND MEMBER OF PARLIAMENT

Now that we've become experts at setting our three levels of priorities, we will now take a look at the three key components of time we draw from during our lives:

- *career*
- *family*
- *self (personal)*

Leadership organizations base their group meetings on these three key areas of focus because they are universal to all of us. By recognizing how our own lives are divided into these same three areas, we can then begin to examine more closely the trade-offs we make with our time. We all have a limited number of hours in the day, and every new commitment we make requires a sacrifice of time from either our career, our family, or our self (personal) component.

Career Time

The time we spend in our career is generally the least flexible of the three components. Regardless of our position within an organization, the professional growth and increased earning potential we seek depend upon dedication to our work and developing trust from the company's leaders. Whether we are climbing the ladder or we own the ladder, neglecting our work responsibilities carries significant risk that can ripple through the other two key areas of our lives. While some individuals may be fortunate to have excess free time at work, the majority of us are simply unable to reliably divert career time for other purposes.

Career time is also considered first because, unless we are independently wealthy, we slice that piece of the pie first. If my current high-level priorities include reaching the highest levels of my firm or industry, I will be required to allocate the majority of my time to my career. My evenings and weekends are likely to be spent working, while family and other interests take a backseat. If, on the other hand, coaching my kids and regularly eating dinner at home are high-level priorities, I have to cut a thinner slice of career time.

Family Time

Family time may be more flexible, but there will still be ramifications when it is abused. The amount of time will vary from person to person due to variables including marital status, number of children, health challenges, and the current stage of life. A single adult without children will typically have the smallest family time component, unless they have a parent or sibling requiring special needs. Likewise, a married person with young children will have a larger family time component than an empty nester.

Self (Personal) Time

Self time is everything remaining after our career and family components have been accounted for. It includes our social lives, entertainment, education, and hobbies. It includes volunteer work, self-improvement, and even developing new potential business ideas. Self time is by far the most flexible of our time components, and the one we are most likely to draw from first when making new voluntary commitments. As such, it is also the easiest to waste.

The key point I'd like to make with respect to our three time components is that, once we've selected our career path and the type of family we'll have, we often don't get to determine the time allocations for either. Those are set for us by the expectations of others. This is one of the great disconnects in our thinking and can frequently lead to disappointment or outright resentment. Put simply, it looks like this: my employer sets my career time, my spouse and kids set my family time, and the remainder is my self (personal) time. When I don't reallocate time away from my career, I keep those at work happy. When I don't reallocate time away from my family, I keep those at home happy. Guess where I get into the most trouble?

More often than not, it is our family time that suffers. Generally this happens because whatever time we add to our self component must be taken from somewhere else, and our careers just aren't quite as flexible. For this reason, we always want to take advantage of those opportunities to combine self with family or career whenever we can. For example: playing golf with a business customer or taking the kids on a fishing trip.

The ideal work/life balance is one in which everyone's expectations are aligned: We work as much as expected, we are present with our family as expected, and most importantly, we ourselves are as happy as expected. Maintaining this balance is key to getting the most out of our lives. If our mismanagement of any of the three time components is creating friction with another, we need to make some changes.

5

What Will Be Your Legacy?

People will forget what you said,
people will forget what you did,
but people will never forget
how you made them feel.

—MAYA ANGELOU,
AMERICAN CIVIL RIGHTS ACTIVIST

Time is our greatest asset, but we never know when it will run out. One day we will be gone, and the world will continue on without us. Some of us will be forgotten while others will be unforgettable. What we do with our time, how we've lived our lives, and whose hearts we've touched—that is how we will be remembered. That is our legacy.

In early March 2020, NBA legend Charles Barkley announced he was going to be selling off his trophies, Olympic medals, and his 1993 Most Valuable Player award. The headline got people's attention, but this wasn't another sad story about a professional athlete who squandered his millions of dollars and had gone broke. The reason Sir Charles was selling a Hall of Fame career's worth of accolades: to build affordable housing in his hometown of Leeds, Alabama.

My son, Noah, typically the first to break any sports news to me, couldn't believe it, "Why in the world would he sell off these rare items?" For kids who collect trophies, autographs, and sports memorabilia, it's unfathomable that a legend like Sir Charles would consider relinquishing these one-of-a-kind artifacts. If he didn't want them, perhaps his daughter or grandkids would. What I understood immediately, and appreciated the opportunity to explain to Noah, was that Barkley saw an opportunity to leverage those mementos into making a real difference in people's lives. He was continuing to grow his legacy.

Charles Barkley spent sixteen years playing in the NBA. He was an eleven-time NBA All-Star and had his jerseys retired by Auburn University, the Phoenix Suns, and the Philadelphia 76ers. He also earned two Olympic gold medals for Team USA. Reaching that level of success would have been more than enough for any man to live off for the rest of his life. But Barkley was not content with basketball greatness as his legacy. He transitioned successfully to television in 2000 and built a wonderful second career as a studio analyst for TNT. Kids who never even watched him play the game now recognize him for his broadcast work. He has even floated the idea multiple times of getting into politics—yet another brilliant example of effectively adjusting high-level priorities.

Inanimate objects from a former career aren't too important to Charles Barkley. In fact, it might surprise you to know that all the sports memorabilia from his two decades playing have been sitting in storage at his grandmother's home. He originally planned to leave it to his daughter, but she supported Charles's big idea to "do something really nice for Leeds, and if I could build ten to twenty affordable houses—I want to do green housing too. If I could sell all that stuff, it would just be a really cool thing for me." The only thing his daughter asked to keep was the 1992 Olympic gold medal he won as a member of the Dream Team. "See," I jokingly told Noah, "His daughter got something!"

Plenty of iconic athletes will be forever remembered for their incredible achievements within their sport. Others, like Muhammad Ali, have used their celebrity status or access to wealth in order to further humanitarian issues. When most legends walk past their trophy cases of awards and memorabilia earned over a brilliant career, they are reminded they were once part of something special.

What Charles Barkley saw instead was that he could take a bunch of items gathering dust inside one home and transform them into several homes. Those homes, in turn, would transform an entire community. Our legacy is the story of what we did with our time here, and Barkley has continued making the most of his. When we set our own priorities, are there opportunities for us to make an even bigger impact with our time?

6

When Time Runs Out

Show me that the good life
doesn't consist in its length,
but in its use.

—SENECA,
ROMAN PHILOSOPHER

We rarely know when our time is up, and we are never guaranteed another day. Jim Koch, founder of the Boston Beer Company, keeps a telephone message in a frame hanging on his office wall. The message says, "I'll call you back on Monday." Jim's secretary had taken the message for him one Friday when he was out of the office. On Sunday, the thirty-four-year-old man who had called died of a heart attack. Jim keeps the message as a reminder that Monday doesn't always come.

Sometimes it hits even closer to home. Ricky was one of my best friends in high school and a roommate of mine in college. He toasted Stacey and me as a groomsman at our wedding and less than three months later he was gone. After spending Thanksgiving weekend in Chicago, he was tragically killed in a car accident on his way back to Colorado. Ricky's life as an adult had hardly begun, and yet his influence on me had far more impact than he could have known.

37

Ricky got everyone to loosen up and have fun. He showed us all how to make the most of any situation. Once, when we didn't have tickets to a Chicago Blackhawks play-off hockey game, he insisted we listen to the broadcast outside in the cold—just to generate the feeling of being there on the ice. I remember that as fondly as any game I've ever seen in person. He moved to Steamboat Springs to enjoy the mountains and pursue his passion as a chef. He squeezed more life and love out of his twenty-four years here than many people do in three times that length. He was taken from us way too soon, but not before he taught us all the value of appreciating the time we have. He showed us how to live now and not waste any time or energy on things that might never happen. That is his legacy to me.

Tragedy struck Ricky's family again when, just a few years after Ricky's death, his older sister Jody suddenly fell ill and passed away from a rare illness. She left behind a husband and two young children. No parent should ever have to bury a child, but for Steve and Sheila to do it twice was unfathomable. There is a saying that God will never put you through anything you can't handle. He put my friend's parents through hell. However, they are not only remarkable because they endured these unimaginable heartbreaks. Despite all they'd lost, they continued to find ways to make the most of their time for the loved ones still around them.

This was the family I spent countless evenings with throughout much of high school. There were always friends around the dinner table and a fresh tray of Sheila's cookies (still my favorite) on the counter. Only years later did I hear about their financial challenges during that time period. Yet they continued feeding guests, treating us like family, and always keeping it fun. I never detected even a hint of tension in the house, though they might have been quite concerned about paying the rent. Their fortunes later turned when Steve and Sheila built a successful business together. They bought a nicer house and built a swimming pool where everyone would congregate. It was exactly how karma is supposed to work. Good things should eventually happen to good people.

Instead, two of their children are gone. You could forgive anyone for hating the world and questioning religion after experiencing these twin horrors, but Steve and Sheila would not be broken. Although they certainly grieved and had bouts of anger and frustration, they also realized there were two other children and several grandchildren living their lives who loved them and enjoyed their company. They found a way to move on, without moving past Ricky and Jody. They will never be forgotten and will always remain a part of the family. But the family still remains. Steve and Sheila have chiseled a legacy of uncommon strength and perseverance, of taking everything life threw at them, and never letting it crush their spirits. They are a shining example of valuing time and setting priorities through the very worst of circumstances.

"I was blessed. I was told I had three months to live," is how Eugene O'Kelly began his memoir, *Chasing Daylight*. O'Kelly was the CEO of a multibillion-dollar company when he was diagnosed with advanced terminal brain cancer. He was only fifty-two years old with a wife, two daughters, and a seemingly limitless future. And it was all about to end in a matter of months. "The quicker I scrapped plans for a life that no longer existed, the better," he said. "I needed to come up with new goals. Fast."

O'Kelly's goals for the remaining three months of his life were to "beautifully resolve" all his relationships and create as many special moments as possible with those closest to him. Through phone calls or e-mails to acquaintances, and dinners with close friends, O'Kelly focused on making each interaction enjoyable and expressing his appreciation for the relationship. Shortly before his death, he wrote, "I experienced more Perfect

Moments and Perfect Days in two weeks than I had in the last five years, or than I probably would have in the next five years, had my life continued the way it was going before my diagnosis."

Rather than lamenting his life being cut short, O'Kelly chose to be grateful for receiving a three-month warning. He immediately got to work, setting his new priorities of tying up loose ends and spending quality time with the people he cared most about. Chip and Dan Heath share O'Kelly's story in their book *The Power of Moments* to emphasize how it isn't the amount of time we have left, but what we choose to do with it that really enriches us. None of us need to develop a terminal illness to appreciate the things that truly matter most.

You only live once? False. You live every day.
You only die once.

—DWIGHT SCHRUTE,
PLAYED BY ACTOR
RAINN WILSON IN *THE OFFICE*

There are very few positives about attending a funeral, but it does offer the constructive periodic reminder that time eventually runs out for all of us. A funeral gets us thinking about how we might be remembered when it is our turn to be the guest of honor. Pay attention to the eulogies given at the next funeral you attend and reflect carefully on your own life. Think about the people you spend the most time with and how they will eulogize you when you're gone. Those who know us best should have the most to say. And yet how sad is it when a speaker cannot relay a funny story or detail a noteworthy accomplishment? Did the deceased live an unremarkable life, or was it spent with these boring individuals unable to articulate how this person changed their world? I consider either of these circumstances to be unfortunate.

One of the most challenging tasks I've ever faced was giving the eulogy at my dad's funeral without falling apart. We had our ups and downs, but he meant the world to me. He lived life in a big way, and there was no shortage of stories from his friends for me to draw from, one crazier than the next. He was funny, he loved creating memories for other people, and he made sure you remembered him. "Your dad was one of a kind," is what so many people told me that day. He certainly was, but so is every one of us. I know he would have appreciated hearing the things I said, and I keep that experience in mind when I think about my own life. I hope I leave my kids enough great material for when their time comes to deliver my eulogy. What do you think yours would say?

Action Exercise

Write your own eulogy. This was an eye-opening exercise that I did once, and I strongly recommend it.

What would those who know you best say about you?

What are the incredible moments in your life?

What are your most meaningful accomplishments?

How do you want to be remembered?

Read it back to yourself. Are you happy with it? Is something missing? Think of this exercise as a State of the Union on your life. The good news is that you still have plenty of time to rewrite that story before it's finalized.

7

Commitments

*It takes twenty years to build a reputation
and five minutes to ruin it.*

—Warren Buffett,
American investor

As I have suggested, we know our time is allocated among three main components: career, family, and self (personal). We know we have to prioritize our time within each component in order to reach our goals. Now we take a closer look at the decisions we make with respect to commitments and how they impact this time structure we've thoughtfully put in place.

Honoring Commitments

I will assume that if you are reading this book you are an individual with good moral character. If I am correct in that assumption then it likely follows that when you make a commitment to anyone or anything you plan to keep it. When we make commitments, we are not only attaching our reputation to something but we are also locking ourselves into an obligation of time.

As depicted in the Venn diagram earlier in the book, our most meaningful experiences often involve the overlap of the three things that matter most: time, relationships, and money. Those meaningful experiences where we maximize all three always involve honoring some commitment to ourselves or to others. This ties directly into the concept of our legacy and how people will remember us. The following two stories about honoring commitments are very close to my heart, and both illustrate how powerful it can sometimes be just to do the right thing.

After my dad's funeral, the father of one of my closest friends pulled me aside. Norm told me, "I want to tell you a story that sums up the kind of person your dad was." It was years ago, before I'd even become friends with his son Rich. Norm had hired my dad's company to build his swimming pool. At that time, my dad's younger brother had been a partner in the business, and my uncle was the one who sold Norm his pool. Unfortunately, Norm's pool was completed with some minor cosmetic imperfections some people might not have even noticed.

My uncle suggested to Norm that he enjoy the pool for a little while and see if the defects continued to bother him. Recognizing that repairing the issue would be a major project to fix a minor problem, Norm reluctantly agreed. As he told me, "I probably would have been fine leaving it, even though it didn't look completely right." A short time later, my dad stopped by Norm's house to inspect his company's work personally. He took a single lap around the deck, looked up at Norm and said, "This looks like shit. We're ripping this up and doing it over."

As I have mentioned, time is our greatest asset, followed by relationships and then money. My dad knew the time it would take to repair Norm's swimming pool as well as the time impact to other projects they were working on. He also knew the money it would cost to do the work. But relationships and reputation were very important to him, which is why my dad always honored his commitments. Once the right thing to do was clear in his mind, he didn't hesitate, even when it contradicted his own brother's position. He was simply honoring the same commitment he made to every customer to build the same quality pool he would put in his own backyard. If a single decision like my dad's left a lasting impression on Norm thirty years later, it is well worth considering our approach to the commitments in our lives today.

I learned the value of honoring commitments from my parents, and I've tried to model that behavior for my children. They are never too young to understand that when we accept an obligation we are both pledging our time and dedicating ourselves to others who are counting on us. My son, Noah, felt the costs of making a big commitment at a young age, as you will see in this next story.

Noah found himself on the Eagles, a select baseball team of ten-year-olds that had five parent coaches. As those of you familiar with the insanity of youth sports can relate to, the coaches' kids were frequently prioritized, regardless of ability or performance. Noah and other players sat far more than they deserved to, and it was obvious to many of the parents. Noah hid his disappointment and continued to work hard. He remained positive and supportive, despite the fact that neither the time he dedicated to practicing nor his actual performance were fairly rewarded.

When the state tournament arrived at the end of the season, the coaches suddenly made some changes. Noah and another kid, who had also sat much of the season, found themselves in the starting lineups. Noah even happened to be the starting pitcher for the only two games the Eagles won in the tournament. Surprisingly, some of the coaches' kids didn't play much at all.

Noah had felt dejected and unappreciated throughout much of the long season, but this late vote of confidence from the coaches washed that away. While Stacey and I were still upset about the overall way he'd been treated, we agreed to let him return for a second season with the Eagles. Sadly, the expanded role he expected, and felt he earned, did not materialize.

Once again, Noah found himself playing behind the coaches' kids. Early in the season, he realized he'd made a mistake coming back. Rather than quit, or express any disappointment, he continued to make every practice, work hard, and do whatever was asked of him. Near the end of another long and trying season, Noah was ready to move on. Just prior to the Eagles' second state tournament, Noah privately tried out for, and was invited to join, an even higher-level team for the next season. Just one last tournament with the Eagles and Noah's commitment to them would be completed.

Noah again was tapped as the starting pitcher for the first game at State, where he threw four no-hit innings to upset the top-seeded team in the tournament. Throughout the weekend, he rarely left the field, and even pitched the Eagles to another victory before they fell just one win short of the championship game. You almost couldn't script a better ending. Except Noah actually did.

Just a couple of days after the season, which had ended on such a high note, Noah came into our bedroom looking very sad. He said, "I know I am supposed to play for this new team next year, but I've thought about it a lot and I don't think I want to play baseball anymore." And just like that, it was all over.

My mind flipped through a slideshow of years spent together in the backyard, at private lessons, and on the practice fields. These meaningful moments all included the powerful overlap of time, relationships, and money. It initially saddened me that after all we had invested together in this sport, I would never get to see him play again. But then I began to see it in a much greater context.

I will always have the videos and memories of Noah playing baseball. But nothing he would ever do on the baseball field could outshine the character and integrity he displayed throughout those two seasons. Even when I could no longer suppress my own frustrations for him, he refused to hurt the team with any negativity. He honored his commitment to the Eagles right up until the day the season ended, even though he felt they had broken their commitment to him. This was one of those special moments in life when you actually learn from your kids.

Both Noah and my dad demonstrated that when we make commitments, we are guaranteeing our time, our reputation, and often our money. They can be rewarding but they can also be costly. Noah's story shows how in order to dedicate ourselves fully to those commitments we are passionate about, we need to be much more discerning about the ones we accept. My dad used to say, "Anything worth doing is worth doing right." That is why we must first determine whether something is worth doing at all.

Refusing Commitments

*Life moves pretty fast. If you don't stop and look
around once in a while, you could miss it.*

—FERRIS BUELLER,
PLAYED BY ACTOR MATTHEW BRODERICK
IN *FERRIS BUELLER'S DAY OFF*

One of the most common regrets later in life is not
having done enough with our time. Another regret is
having tried to do too much with it. When we overcommit
ourselves to activities we aren't passionate about, we risk
missing out on the truly meaningful ones. It's the principle
of opportunity cost once again. To honor our agreements,
we must be much more selective about the ones we make
in order to maximize our time.

Noah maintained his commitment to the Eagles right
up until the season was over. It took a lot for him to
continue working hard under those circumstances, and it
illustrates the risks we take getting stuck in something that
doesn't work out. We were proud of the way he handled
himself during baseball, but we were even prouder of the
way he was willing to risk upsetting us with his decision
to move on. He had already figured out the other side of
the commitment coin: prioritizing our time and saying no
when our heart is not in something. If an eleven-year-old
boy can do it, so can you.

Noah could easily have decided to give baseball
another year, especially with the fresh start on a new
team. But then he would never have had the time to
explore other sports he might enjoy more, like tennis and
golf. He also freed up more time to work on improving
his basketball game, which has always been his first love.
He never would have had those opportunities if he hadn't
created that space in his life.

We all need to maintain space for new possibilities. If
life were a suitcase, would you stuff it completely before

you leave town, or would you leave a little room in it for something unexpected you might find along the way? Scheduling and preparation are essential for success, but it takes discipline to leave a little room for those spontaneous surprises and opportunities. Overloading our calendars limits our flexibility and restricts our ability to change direction. As Stacey Snider, who became the cochairman of 20th Century Fox, learned, "If I hadn't allowed myself to venture off the beaten path, I wouldn't have discovered an enthusiasm for something unexpected." We can't get off the beaten path if we have taken on too much. We have to have the discipline to refuse those commitments we aren't strongly drawn to.

It's all very simple, actually. Our happiness increases when we are engaged in meaningful activities and are available to engage in other meaningful activities we encounter. Everything else should be minimized to whatever extent possible. We've all identified an obvious waste of time at the outset, but for some reason agreed anyway. Once we've determined something isn't worth our time, we need to be done with it. Not everything works out the way we originally planned, but when we limit our commitments to only the opportunities that speak to us, we will enjoy far more magical moments.

8

Saying No

*Half of the troubles of this life
can be traced to saying yes too quickly
and not saying no soon enough.*

—JOSH BILLINGS,
ACTOR AND HUMORIST

If we truly want to manage our commitments and take control of our lives, we have to learn to cut things out. As Greg McKeown wrote in *Essentialism: The Disciplined Pursuit of Less,* "If you don't prioritize your life, someone else will." There are always timesuckers swarming around you, and they aren't interested in your agenda. They will ask and they will take. They will push and they will pull. They will knock you off course and prevent you from accomplishing your goals.

When I was a child, I loved a plaque hanging up in my dad's office, which read, "When you are up to your ass in alligators, it is difficult to remind yourself that your initial objective was to drain the swamp."

Not long ago, I had an exact replica produced for my own office, where it hangs today. It serves as a powerful reminder for me that my priorities are always under attack. If I don't work to set boundaries and limits on my time,

I have no way to protect it. The only effective way to accomplish this is to become proficient at saying no.

Saying Yes by Saying No

In *The Power of a Positive No,* William Ury demonstrates that a no actually begins with a yes: "Yes, I'd like to do *this,* so no, I can't agree to do *that.*" We need to be clear on what is important to us and disciplined enough to screen out what is not. Again, this is addition by subtraction. It's how we make the necessary room in our lives for the things that can be meaningful. Thinking in these terms helps reduce the anxiety or guilt that can drive us into making poor commitment choices.

The stakes are highest when someone familiar to us is asking for our time. We assume our friends and acquaintances expect to have our support and that disappointing them could hurt our relationship. I have found the best way to alleviate this concern is by making a clear distinction between the person and the obligation. I might say, "I really want to support you because I value our friendship, but this is not something I can take on right now. Would you please let me know when you have other opportunities in the future I might consider?"

Always remember two things:

- An opportunity doesn't become an obligation until we accept it.

- Each commitment we accept reduces the time available for everything else we want to do.

We have no choice but to be more selective with our time, and this requires saying no to people we really want to say yes to. Further, as my next story will illustrate, open-ended time commitments are never forever. Organizations are managed by people and, as such, tend to change over time. We may eventually find it appropriate to step away because a group's culture or priorities have diverged too far from our own.

My first meaningful foray into volunteer work began when I was thirty and had just moved to Omaha. A new friend invited me to make solicitation phone calls for an organization's annual fund-raising campaign. It was a one-day telethon that first opened my eyes to the incredible possibilities of what a small group could accomplish working together for a shared goal. Soon after, I joined the organization's board and spent a decade in various roles. I chaired the young leadership group, the big annual fund-raising campaign, and the community gala. I also helped rewrite the organization's bylaws and tackled several other initiatives.

Through the hundreds of hours volunteered, I developed some valuable skills. Those include leading effective meetings, conflict resolution, public speaking, and forging working relationships with other leaders. Simply by agreeing to make a few phone calls one Sunday, I ended up with ten years of personal growth and organizational experience. I was also able to have a positive impact on my community and was proud to be honored with two special awards. It was one of the most meaningful experiences of my life. And yet, one day I abruptly walked away from it.

As I mentioned, people and organizations are constantly evolving. Once I felt we were no longer in alignment, I was simply no longer interested in investing my valuable time. I took the first opportunity to exit gracefully before wearing out my welcome. Had I remained involved, my frustrations would have destroyed much of the goodwill I had contributed over the years. As Dan Hicks famously sang, "How Can I Miss You When You Won't Go Away?"

By effectively saying no, I freed up time to say yes to some exciting new opportunities. I became reenergized by exploring new groups I was interested in working with. I continued growing by setting new and different priorities. All experiences, whether positive or negative, improve us and strengthen us for our next challenge. We just have to recognize when the time is right to make the occasionally uncomfortable decision to move on.

A cautionary note about volunteering: Be aware that those people who show up and come through are placed at the top of the list for the next big ask that comes along. If we don't actively set our boundaries, we won't have any. In our careers, we advance by earning more responsibility and creating more opportunities for ourselves. Paying more dues at work will often pay more bills at home. When it comes to our personal time, however, others tend to get too comfortable leaning on the same people for help. We have to get comfortable saying no, and the next section will help with that.

Action Exercise

Write down a memorable commitment you wish you'd said no to.

Did you help a friend do something?

Did you volunteer to take on a leadership or coaching role?

Did you agree to help organize or manage a function?

Did you join a committee?

What stopped you from declining it?

How would you handle it differently next time?

How to Say No

When it comes to managing our time, there is no more valuable tool than the word no. Our habits, priorities, and commitments are all about determining *what* we need to say no to, and *when.* Now we will spend a little time focusing on *how* we say it.

While I was the president of my fraternity at the University of Kansas, I had to strike a difficult balance between living among the animals and acting as the head zookeeper. Once upon a time, freshmen were relied upon to handle many of the more unpleasant tasks in the fraternity, in essence earning their membership with sweat equity. During my tenure, the rules changed, and we were no longer allowed to force freshmen to perform any activity without the assistance of at least one older member. During all-house cleanups, it was my responsibility to make sure that our upperclassmen were, at the very least, in the vicinity of a broom. This process generally went smoothly, with one notable exception that became folklore among my friends.

I'm disinclined to acquiesce to your request.
It means no.

—CAPTAIN BARBOSSA,
PLAYED BY ACTOR GEOFFREY RUSH
IN *PIRATES OF THE CARIBBEAN:*
CURSE OF THE BLACK PEARL

The head of any organization, including a group of drunken misfits, should lead by example. During an all-house clean-up one Sunday morning, I was cleaning the formal room with several other fraternity brothers. Suddenly, my good friend Corey, who I would expect to feel obliged to help out, strolled right past us into the kitchen. Shamelessly emerging with a full bowl of cereal, he slowly shuffled past us again on his way back to his bedroom. Somewhat stunned and slightly irritated, I barked, "Hey, Corey, would you care to join the rest of us so we can get this house clean?" My outburst prompted him to stop and turn around. But rather than change his mind, he looked directly at me and said, "I'm sorry, Brett. I just don't feel like it." And with that, he continued on his way.

This story has been often retold, primarily to celebrate the humor in Corey's brazen selfishness. Not only did he blow off his share of the labor, but he did it so openly and with such panache. However, he also put me into a managerial quandary: allow my good friend to circumvent the rules or punish him and potentially create a rift between us. Ultimately, I split the difference and asked him to apologize to the rest of the house. It wasn't my proudest moment as a leader, but it wasn't my worst either. I was only twenty years old, after all.

Though Corey will certainly be excited to be included in this book even just for a joke at his expense, that isn't the reason he's here (but feel free to laugh at him; he can take it). While I was less than thrilled with his motivations that morning, I confess that over time I've developed a certain admiration for his resolve. Despite social pressures (dirty looks from his fraternity brothers) and a direct request (from a close friend, no less), he neither wavered nor hesitated for one second. He confidently declined, stated his reason, and continued on his way. Maturity would later bring a greater sense of community into his life, but he had already developed this valuable skill of saying no much sooner than the rest of us.

Corey remains a good friend of mine to this day. He's a terrific husband and father, a successful attorney, and far removed from his twenty-year-old self. However, the ability to say no that he displayed back then has continued to serve him extremely well throughout his life.

Let's break down Corey's Sunday-morning breakfast stroll, which was a textbook case of saying no properly. Like all perfect rejections, Corey's contained the Three Rs:

- Begin with *respect.*
- Give your *response.*
- State your *reason.*

One of our strongest fears about saying no is how it will affect our relationship with the other person. In reality, the way you handle the interaction is more impactful than the answer. If someone has taken the time to make a request of you, it holds some level of importance to them.

They are entitled to your *respect*. Avoiding them or failing to return their phone calls is insulting and sends the message that you think you're more important than they are. Listen to the request with your full attention. It won't take up much of your time at all. Even Corey stopped to hear me out when I asked him to help clean the house!

The next step is to give your *response*. If you need more time to consider the request, just provide a time when you plan to deliver your answer ("I will let you know on Monday morning.") and follow through. Clarify the time commitment, ask any questions you have, and confirm what exactly is expected of you. Gather all the information you need so there are no misunderstandings later. And again, never agree for the wrong reasons.

The last, and most critical, step is to state your *reason*. A mishandled delivery is typically what negatively impacts the relationship. Rather than create confusion or uncertainty around your motives for saying no, it is always best to state your reasoning confidently. Nervousness can arouse suspicion and leave more questions than answers behind. Remember when Corey explained he simply didn't feel like cleaning the house when he was supposed to? Despite being an asinine response, it was genuine and matter-of-factly delivered. There was no further speculation about how he was feeling or what he planned to do. Even in the most ridiculous of circumstances, this is still the proper way to say no.

There is no need to justify the validity of your reasoning, or to be concerned whether or not it will disappoint the other person. You need only respectfully consider the request, make a decision that is true to your goals and priorities, and deliver it confidently. Get comfortable doing that and you can take back control of your time.

Here are a few examples of how you can say no. Each one incorporates the Three Rs—respect, response, and reason.

- That is a very cool thing you're a part of, but unfortunately I have to say no. I can't devote any additional time to volunteer work right now.

- I wish I could. This is a really busy time of the year for me, and I've already had to cut back on things I had planned to do. I'm sorry to have to decline.

- I'm not comfortable accepting this because I know I won't be able to devote my full attention to it right now, which wouldn't be fair to either of us. I feel bad but I have to say no.

- I really appreciate what you're doing, but I'm just not the best fit for what you're asking, so I'm going to have to pass on it. Thank you for thinking of me.

- I'm sorry to say no, because I like you and I'd really like to help, but unfortunately this particular opportunity isn't for me.

Each of these responses is simple and respectful. They all convey a firm decision made without overexplaining or vacillating. You can also incorporate a rain check by saying, "If something else comes up, please consider asking me again." This closes on a very positive note and leaves the other person feeling they can still count on you at a later date. But short of saying "I'm sorry" once more if the person starts begging (a rare occurrence), the conversation is over.

Action Exercise ·

Practice saying no until you become comfortable and confident doing it.

Welcome the opportunity to decline a few solicitations in stores and restaurants (unless you genuinely support the cause).

Role-play a few different scenarios with a friend or your spouse. Have them ask you to donate or volunteer.

---

we actually gave our full attention to what we were doing and who we were with.

It happened gradually, but we are now fully immersed in constant connectivity. We literally bump into each other because we are paying more attention to our screens than to the people around us. We are in a perpetual state of communication: texting, posting, tweeting, snapping, sharing, and occasionally holding our phones up to our ears to talk. We are living science fiction, existing both here and there simultaneously. Societal norms have relaxed, fundamentally altering forever what it means to spend time together.

Technological innovation has revolutionized several industries, but it does not always translate into an improved human experience. Take nuclear energy, for example. A key benefit cited by proponents of nuclear power has been the net positive effect on the environment. Yet residents of Pripyat in 1986 might disagree, after fallout from the accidental explosion at the nearby Chernobyl nuclear plant destroyed their landscape along with many lives. My wife, Stacey, has a favorite expression, "Just because you can doesn't mean you should." Smartphones and tablets have made it so we can be available to anyone at any time and any place. But should we be? These devices have put so much power in the palms of our hands, few of us stop to ask, "What might that power actually be destroying?"

Michael Harris attacked this question head-on in his thought-provoking book *The End of Absence.* He and I belong to the last generation that remembers what life was actually like before the Internet, before cell phones, before being constantly connected to a network that never sleeps. We now have instant access to whatever information we need. We don't ever have to worry about being lost. We can shop from anywhere in the world. We can record pictures or videos of anything. These are only a few of the time-saving benefits of owning a smartphone, and we have conditioned ourselves to reach for it immediately whenever we want anything.

However, while so much productivity has been gained by these advancements, so many of our vital and simple pleasures have been lost. We used to have gaps in our schedules that allowed us to think, to process, and to dream. We used to be able to focus for long periods of time without interruption. We used to expect, and accept, that people would be unreachable sometimes. We used to be fully present with other human beings because time spent with them was meaningful. As we have continued stuffing our lives with more and more of everything, the moments we spend with those we care about become more and more precious.

Sometimes you will never know the value of a moment until it becomes a memory.

—DR. SEUSS,
AMERICAN CHILDREN'S AUTHOR

Instead of utilizing the power of the smartphone for its intended purpose—to free up more time for our real lives—we've allowed the device itself to be an intruder into everything we do. We have literally opened a portal that keeps half of our mind somewhere else. Every chime or vibration interrupts a meal, a meaningful conversation, a *moment*. Unnecessary distractions degrade the quality of every interaction we have. They make it impossible to remain on task, disrupting any flow we expected to have. It's no wonder anxiety, depression, and attention deficit disorder are so prevalent in our society. How can we call this "progress" when it consistently diminishes the value and meaning of our experiences?

We've voluntarily tied wireless leashes around our necks. Most of us would be perfectly fine catching up on our messages at set intervals throughout our day. Then again, most of us don't. The people who truly value their time are able to set boundaries on their smartphone use. They don't answer every e-mail, text message, or phone call immediately when it arrives. They set their phones aside while they're spending time with family and friends. Breaking news alerts will still be waiting for them later.

There are different ways to begin changing our smartphone habits, and I've seen some executed very well. An acquaintance has an auto-reply on his e-mail saying, "In an effort to remain focused, I will be checking my e-mail at set intervals throughout the day. Thank you for your patience." Another posted to Facebook, "Please understand I check social media only periodically, so I may not see or respond to everything." One of my friends sent a group text message saying, "I'm planning to cut back on the time I spend on my phone, so don't be upset if I don't text right back. If it's important, please call me." Once we've trained others on how we structure our priorities, and we remain consistent, our boundaries will be respected.

It takes discipline to break the habit of constantly being on call for everyone and everything, particularly in a world where rampant smartphone use has become acceptable. Changing my device habits has been a struggle with occasional relapses. Through the process, I have felt a deepening enjoyment of my time, which motivates me to continue working at it. I relish getting lost in the moment again. I savor long conversations over a glass of bourbon. I take great pleasure in watching my kids experience life rather than clearing my inbox. I have begun to better appreciate the things that truly matter.

Smartphone reform provides the perfect bridge from the study of time into the study of relationships, the next major section of the book. The way we use our smartphones not only has a significant impact on the quality of our time, but on the quality of our relationships as well. We have to learn to control our phones instead of letting them control us.

> ## Action Exercise
>
> Begin a one-week smartphone detox program.
>
> *For one week, leave your phone in your pocket when you're with other people. Fight the urge to pull it out.*
>
> *Make it a habit to live in the moment and save the texting, e-mail, and social media for when you're alone again.*
>
> *Begin disabling the alerts and notifications you don't need.*
>
> *After one week, reflect on your experience. Were there any noticeable changes? How do you feel? Can you keep it going?*

Time: Summary

Because we cannot stop or slow the endless passing of time, we often take for granted how precious it really is. Our days flow into weeks, our weeks into months, and our months into years. Locked into our routines, cruising on autopilot, we miss out on so many opportunities to enrich our lives before they end. Consider the story of the professor and the boatman:

One day, a professor was being rowed across a wide river in a boat. Since the man liked to hear himself talk, he asked the boatman, "Do you understand math and science?"

"No," said the boatman. "I have never had time to learn such things."

"You poor man," said the professor. "You have wasted a quarter of your life. If you knew math and science, you would be better off. Have you read the classics?"

"No," answered the boatman humbly. "I wasn't able to finish school. I needed to work to feed my family. I never learned to read very well and haven't read the classics."

"Too bad," said the professor. "You have lost half of your life. Reading would have served you well. Have you traveled to other countries?"

"No," said the boatman. "I have spent my whole life here on the river."

The professor sneered. "You have lost three quarters of your life. Only by traveling can you live life to the fullest. You should have stayed in school and received a proper education."

Then it was the boatman's turn. He turned and asked the professor, "Can you swim?"

"No," answered the professor. "I spent my youth in the classroom studying math, science, and the classics. I have spent my adulthood teaching and traveling. I did not find frolicking in the water to be an endeavor worth pursuing."

"Oh, that's a shame." said the boatman, smiling. "Then I fear you have lost your whole life. For the boat is sinking."

As the professor discovered the hard way, how we choose to spend our time impacts our lives more than anything else.

Let's quickly summarize the ideas we just covered concerning time.

- The three things that matter most are time, relationships, and money. When we value them all properly, we will experience our most meaningful moments. This is the area of the diagram where they overlap.

- Time is our greatest asset. We can never earn it back.

- Do anything enough—good or bad—and it becomes a habit.

- Eating the elephant requires setting priorities from the top down.

- High-level priorities are the most important things in our lives.
- Intermediate priorities are the big milestones along the way.
- Short-term priorities are our daily activities.

- Our biggest regrets later in life will be the things we didn't do.
- Our time is broken into three components: career, family, and self (personal). Every new commitment we make requires time pulled from one of them.
- What will be your legacy after you are gone? Are you happy with the stories that will be told at your funeral?
- In order to honor our commitments fully, we have to focus on the ones we are passionate about.
- Spend time doing things that are meaningful and keep time available for other things that might be meaningful.
- Saying no is addition by subtraction. Remove the things that don't add value to our lives in order to make room for those that will.
- Get comfortable saying no with the three Rs:
  - Begin with *respect.*
  - Give our *response.*
  - State our *reason.*
- Our mobile devices are for our convenience. They work for us, not the other way around.

As we move through the next sections of the book, the concept of time will remain ever present. I believe prioritizing our time has the single biggest impact on reaching our goals. Even when we fail to stay on track completely, the continual effort drives us so much further down the road than if we just sit back and let life happen.

We spend the majority of our time focusing on the tasks we need to accomplish from day to day, but we seldom step back and view our lives as a whole. Our legacy is the story of our life, and that story will ultimately be told by others. How will you be remembered? What do you hope to be celebrated for? What do you hope is forgotten? With those questions in mind, we now move on to the second-most valuable asset we have—our relationships.

Part II

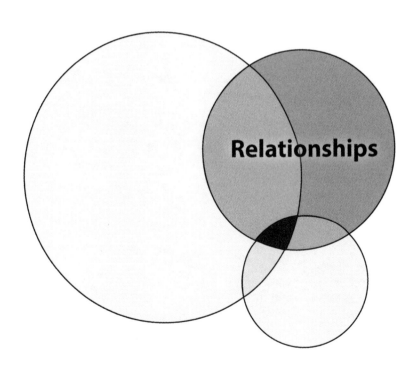

Relationships

10

It's Not What, but Whom

Life is partly what we make it,
and partly what it is made
by the friends we choose.

—TENNESSEE WILLIAMS,
AMERICAN PLAYWRIGHT

In Part I, we established that time is our most valuable asset and that we need to prioritize it accordingly. We now turn our attention toward the people we choose to invest that time in. Life is a shared experience, which places monumental importance on the choices we make about other people. By the same token, we need to remain aware how the courses of our lives are hugely impacted by decisions others make about us.

To illustrate the value of life as a shared experience, consider the following story.

A wealthy man lived in the biggest house on the nicest block of a large town. He had every luxury you could imagine, and he never wasted an opportunity to tell people about it.

His young son, who had been studying abroad, returned home for a visit. The wealthy man wanted to impress his son with how rich he was and how proud the son should be to have him as a father. The man took his son on a two-day tour of the countryside, to show the boy how the poor people live.

On the way back home, the father noticed that his son was sullen and quiet after experiencing the conditions of the people out in the country.

The wealthy man asked, "Well, my son, have you enjoyed our time together?"

"Yes father," the boy replied, "I had a great time."

"So, did you notice how poor people live?" the father asked.

"Yes, I sure did," replied the boy.

The father asked his son to tell him more.

"Well," the boy explained, "we have a big pool in our garden, but they have a huge lake that never ends. With so much water, they can spend their days swimming, fishing, and kayaking together all at the same time.

We have expensive light fixtures imported from different countries, but they have countless stars that fill the sky above them at night. They spend their evenings talking and laughing together underneath them outside.

We have a house on a small piece of land, but they have fields that stretch to the horizon. There is no limit to the games they can play out there.

We buy our food from the store, but they are able to grow their own food and trade with each other. They never run out of anything they want to eat.

We have big walls and a fence to keep us safe, but they have no need for those because their friends protect them."

The wealthy man was stunned into silence.

"Dad," the boy continued, "Thank you so much for letting me see how poor we are."

The son quickly perceived how true wealth is not measured by the things we have but rather by the quality of our relationships. They are vital to our well-being, our life experiences, and ultimately what we accomplish with our time. Further, by avoiding negative relationships, we enable ourselves to truly grow. Before considering our acquaintances, friends, and families, however, we will first explore the most important relationship we will ever have: *the one with ourselves.*

11

Me, Myself, and I

Knowing yourself is the beginning of all wisdom.

—ARISTOTLE,
GREEK PHILOSOPHER

Every relationship we choose to have throughout our lives is a product of how closely we understand ourselves. We gravitate toward those with whom we instinctively feel compatible and connected, but that doesn't always mean we are surrounding ourselves with the right people. The better we become at knowing who we are, what we really want, and why we feel the way we do, the more we will improve our key relationships.

Because we are all constantly evolving, the ability to understand ourselves at different points in our lives is essential. In his autobiography, musician Jeff Tweedy related an analogy between people and wood. He said we should always think of ourselves as the tree, not the table. Whereas the table is all it will ever be, the tree never stays the same. We are all on our own unique journeys. In *Emotional Equations,* Chip Conley wrote, "The most important challenge might be in finding the willingness to give up who you think you are in order to find out who you might become." None of us is a finished product. When we develop the self-awareness to know who we are now and what we want to become, we can throw off the chains keeping us from getting there.

How well do you really know yourself? What kind of priority is that relationship for you? How much time and effort do you actually spend working on it? Each of us has a few key dials we need to focus on adjusting. As we work to understand and improve these areas within ourselves, we will notice all the relationships in our lives vastly improve. The way others view us is a direct function of the way we view others, and that all begins with taking a look at our perspective.

Adjusting Our Perspective

We don't see things as they are,
we see them as we are.

—ANAÏS NIN,
FRENCH-CUBAN-AMERICAN WRITER

Our perspective is the individual way in which each of us interprets the world around us. Author David Foster Wallace provided one of the best explanations of perspective during his 2005 speech at Kenyon College's graduation:

There are two young fish swimming along, and they happen to meet an older fish swimming the other way, who nods at them and says, "Morning, boys, how's the water?" And the two young fish swim on for a bit, and then eventually one of them looks over at the other and goes, "What the hell is water?"

The older fish, of course, has total awareness of his surroundings, while the young fish have been completely oblivious to what is so essential and hiding in plain sight all around them. Similarly, we all live in the same world and breathe the same air, but we can see it all very differently. Though we may be part of the exact same experience, it may have a very different meaning to each of us.

Perspective is a powerful lens that can enhance or distort what we see and how we interpret it. Adjusting that lens will often mean the difference between happiness or misery in the very same set of circumstances. We often forget how much of life is out of our direct control, yet we continue to punish ourselves and blame others unnecessarily. Each day that goes by is another chunk of our precious time lost forever, while we continue taking all our blessings for granted.

Faulty perceptions prevent some of us from recognizing that the time we have each day is a gift. As a result, we find different ways to waste it. By properly setting goals and priorities, we guide ourselves toward meaningful accomplishments. Our perspective plays a vital role in the process. It allows us to find true meaning in the pursuit of those accomplishments, rather than what the end results might be. American essayist and poet Ralph Waldo Emerson reportedly said, "Life is a journey, not a destination."

Proper perspective reminds us we will all arrive at the same destination when life is over. To emphasize this point, the Roman emperor Marcus Aurelius liked to point out that the Greek king Alexander the Great was buried in the same ground as his mule driver. By remembering that none of us are alive to celebrate when we cross our life's finish line, we can derive more pleasure from the ways we spend our days.

Perhaps no book captures the incredible power of perspective better than Viktor Frankl's *Man's Search for Meaning*. It is a terrifying account of his firsthand experiences as a prisoner in multiple concentration camps during World War II. Frankl had his freedoms and his possessions stripped away and watched his entire family perish. Through it all, he still concluded that life always has meaning, even while we are enduring the most extreme suffering possible. There will always be someone who loves and needs us, whether today or in the future.

Imagine the inner strength required just to retain your spirit and your identity when everything else has been taken from you. Imagine summoning the will to believe life can still be beautiful while trapped inside that hell. Now, take a deep breath and consider how irritated you got when the restaurant made a mistake with your order or the driver in front of you forgot to use their turn signal. That is perspective.

Interestingly enough, this was all figured out long before our time. Centuries ago, the ancient Stoic philosophers had already solved many of the problems we continue wrestling with today. Author Ryan Holiday has delivered the teachings of Seneca, Epictetus, and Marcus Aurelius to the modern era, where they remain no less indispensable.

In *The Obstacle Is the Way,* Holiday sums up the essential Stoic insight on perspective: "We decide what we will make of each and every situation." We can seldom prevent most things from happening, but we always have the power to decide what they mean and how we feel about them. The exact same event can ruin our day or roll off our shoulders, but it is going to happen regardless. It is up to each of us to determine whether we accept and address the reality or we lament it and spit into the wind.

In *Stumbling on Happiness,* psychologist Daniel Gilbert suggests that "perceptions are portraits, not photographs, and their form reveals the artist's hand every bit as much as it reflects the things portrayed." In other words, we don't always paint what we see; we paint what we feel. Proper perspective is understanding that we have control only over ourselves. We cannot account for the thoughts, motivations, and actions of others. Yet we allow ourselves to feel threatened, slighted, or irritated in reaction to someone else's decision that doesn't actually affect us at all.

When someone begins complaining to me, there are three questions I will ask them in order to reframe their perspective:

- Does this matter directly affect your life in some way?

- Is there an action you can take to improve the situation?

- What benefit is there for you to be upset about it?

If the person answers no to the first two questions, they have already begun moving past the lingering concern. Get into the habit of saying, "I choose not to be upset about that because it doesn't affect me." Over time, we will develop a shield that actively deflects those nuisances before they get under our skin. It prevents us from wasting precious time and potentially damaging our relationships. Perspective is a skill that can be developed with practice and repetition just like shooting a basketball.

One of the most harmful threats to our perspective is envy. There is a reason it is one of the seven deadly sins. Being overly impressed with what other people appear to have devalues all the wonderful blessings in our own lives. No matter how many rungs we climb on the ladder of success, there are always people above us. When we focus on them, we forget all that we've accomplished with our own time. When a multimillionaire suffers from hypertension while his middle-class chauffeur happily whistles show tunes every day, which of them has the healthier perspective? Allowing envy to fester is a bad habit but, like all habits, it can be broken. Our well-being and the quality of our relationships depend on it.

Envy is a symptom of using the wrong yardstick to measure our happiness. The only person we should be comparing ourselves to is the one staring back at us in the mirror. Am I happier and better off than that person used to be? Yet when someone we know finds good fortune, we may foolishly allow it to put us in a bad mood. Our station in life suddenly feels minimized, and all the wonderful things we have to be grateful for are now worth less to us, simply because a friend built a new house or took an exotic vacation.

Is it not tragically ironic when we are entertained by the lives of random celebrities but upset when someone we care about finds success? Whether they get a big promotion, their business takes off, or they start getting attention from different circles of people, why would we have negative feelings about it? Unchecked envy leads to *schadenfreude,* which is the pleasure derived from another person's misfortune. Seeing someone else knocked down a peg may make us feel better about ourselves by comparison, but it does literally nothing to improve our actual situation.

Another person's success has no effect on our own life at all but it can still feel like something huge has shifted in the universe. We feel threatened because we have lost our perspective about who we are and what is important to us. We fear falling behind, or being left behind, and our envy corrodes what used to be an otherwise positive relationship. While money and success can occasionally change a person, more often than not it changes the people around them.

Thankfully, it doesn't always play out this way, because when we prioritize understanding ourselves better, we develop the ability to catch our faulty perspective and snap it back into proper alignment. We pause to imagine ourselves in the other person's shoes. Wouldn't we be pretty happy and excited to experience the same good fortune? Wouldn't we want others to be happy for us, too? The danger in comparing ourselves to those close to us is that someone always loses.

Success is not a zero-sum game, where another person's gain means we lose. Perhaps it just isn't our turn yet. If our relationship was never based on money or success, then nothing material has actually changed between us. We support our friends and family members when they experience hardships. Do they not deserve our applause and enthusiasm when they succeed? The Buddhist practice of *mudita,* joy in the good fortune of others, is one of the highest four qualities of the heart. When we adjust our perspective to experience happiness for other people, we open the door and invite it into our own lives.

In today's connected world, our efforts to maintain a healthy perspective is constantly under attack by the most effective negative feedback loop ever invented: social media. We need only scroll to experience vicariously all the fabulous lives being lived around us. Everyone appears to be living a dream, primarily because it isn't fully reality. Social media is largely a carefully curated highlight reel: cocktail glasses reflecting the glare of the sunset on the ocean, the family bike ride in the mountains, and the VIP room at a fancy gala.

What we don't see are spouses sleeping in separate rooms after another fight, drugs the perfect child is hiding in the underwear drawer, or the therapist holding the family together. Social media's illusion forces us to compare our average days with everyone else's best days, and we usually come up short. If avoiding social media altogether isn't an option, at least maintain a healthy perspective about it. Remember you are only seeing a scene, not the whole movie.

We need to focus only on the things we can control and ignore what we cannot. Those close to us are on our team; they aren't the competition. If I just shot the best round of golf in my life, is that accomplishment diminished for me because my friend got a better score? Should I be upset with him? Of course not. Am I progressing toward my own goals? Am I better than I used to be? That is what matters. We cannot allow the success of others to negatively impact our own self-worth, especially when we care about them. This is how we lay the foundation, the healthy perspective within ourselves, upon which to build our deepest and most meaningful relationships.

Identify those events that have little to do with your own life but still upset you. Make it a habit to adjust your perspective accordingly and let those things go. Learn to say, "I'm happy for..." when you begin to feel envious of someone in your life.

Action Exercise

Spend a few days noticing when the actions of others generate negative feelings. Write them down in your journal.

Were you excluded from something?

Did you become envious of something you saw?

Did you feel like complaining about a decision someone else made?

Our perspective allows us to better manage many of the negative emotions and habits that can interfere with addressing our priorities. Just as we intentionally determine our priorities, so, too, can we decide what to do with our feelings. We can develop the habit of stepping back and asking ourselves, "Is the way I'm feeling likely to help me to resolve this issue or make it worse?"

Managing Anger and Resentment

Anger is a normal reaction. It's what you do with anger that makes a difference in your life.

—RUDY RUETTIGER,
AMERICAN FOOTBALL PLAYER
AND MOTIVATIONAL SPEAKER

Anger has a bad reputation, but it is actually a natural human emotion that enables us to deal with stress and frustration. Anger only turns negative when we mismanage it, either by suppressing it and hurting ourselves or by projecting it and hurting someone else. The healthy way for us to deal with anger is to recognize it, express it, and address it without losing control of our disposition.

In a classic Zen story, a man is enjoying himself on a river at dusk when he notices another boat coming down the river toward him. At first, he is glad to see someone else enjoying the river on a nice summer evening. Then he realizes the boat is heading right toward him, faster and faster. He begins to yell, "Hey, hey, watch out! For Pete's sake, get out of the way!" But the boat continues racing toward him faster and faster. By this time, he's standing up in his boat, screaming and shaking his fist, when the boat smashes right into him. Only then does he see the other boat is empty.

Anger comes on suddenly and threatens our control over our perspective. Even when nothing has actually been directed at us, we react as if someone intended to do us harm. Consider the man on the river, who was too consumed by his fury at an empty boat to take control of his situation. Who exactly was he angry with? He was the only person who could have avoided the danger, since there wasn't another person around It is the perfect metaphor for how we mismanage our anger a great deal of the time.

I often recall a childhood memory from a ride in my dad's car with both of my siblings. The stoplight turned green, but the car in front of us didn't move. Not only did my dad honk, but he also yelled loudly at the other driver—with our windows closed! The other driver was not intentionally trying to anger my dad, but there was no way he would have heard the yelling regardless. The car in front of us was like the empty boat, and my dad was like the man on the river. While the other driver pulled away unaware, my siblings and I bore the brunt of my dad's unnecessary frustration.

Former UK prime minister Winston Churchill demonstrated a better way to handle anger. According to author Erik Larson, Churchill had an intense hatred of the sound of whistling.

Once, while out walking with Inspector Thompson from Scotland Yard, the pair encountered a young boy "hands in pockets, newspapers under his arms, whistling loudly and cheerfully," as Thompson recalled.

As the boy got closer, Churchill's anger overcame him. "Stop that whistling," he demanded.

The boy, totally unfazed, calmly replied, "Why should I?"

"Because I don't like it and it's a horrible noise."

The boy continued on, turned, and shouted back, "Well, you can shut your ears, can't you?" And the boy continued walking.

Churchill's anger flared up, but after a few more steps he began to smile. He repeated the boy's comment out loud and burst into laughter.

The boy was certainly not whistling to annoy the prime minister, and Churchill's initial reaction was downright absurd. However, though we cannot stop anger from forming inside us, we can work to improve what we do with it.

Churchill was able to change his perspective quickly, turning a disagreeable encounter into a humorous one. How many opportunities like this do we squander every week, and at what cost to our mood and our stress level?

Controlling our anger is often a matter of differentiating between genuine threat or harm and minor irritation or annoyance. Take, for example, our unrealistic expectations of a perfect travel experience every time. Once I was boarding a flight home after a long work trip. Mentally and physically exhausted, I was in no mood to welcome the significantly overweight man who happened to be seated next to me. From the moment he sat down and infringed on my space, my blood began boiling. Doing little to mask my irritation, I agonized over how I could be placed in such an unfair situation. "I paid for a seat," I thought to myself, "not three-quarters of a seat."

Shortly after takeoff, I realized the ridiculousness of my behavior. First, there's nothing I could have done to prevent it from happening, and certainly nothing I could do at that point to change it. Second, I didn't know anything about this man or his life. What if I were in his shoes and had to deal with jerks like me whenever I had to travel? How comfortable could he be, crammed into that little seat? Third, I considered the bigger picture. Yes, I was slightly uncomfortable, but I was literally inside a giant metal tube, safely taking me through the clouds from Detroit to Omaha in just a few hours. On balance, I was doing okay that day.

It suddenly seemed silly for me to punish both of us, when neither of us was truly at fault. I turned to the man and said, "I really owe you an apology. I was irritable when I got on the plane and I was completely rude to you. I'm sorry." And with that, we began a very nice conversation, shared some laughs, and passed the rest of our time together more pleasantly and with significantly lower blood pressures. All it took was a new perspective about my feelings.

The Greek philosopher Epictetus said, "When you get angry, you've not only experienced that evil, but you've also reinforced a bad habit, adding fuel to the fire." Think about how much unnecessary stress each of us could remove from our lives if we made it a habit to stop and ask ourselves, "Is this something I should remain angry about?" If the answer is no, then we should take a deep breath and begin to ease the tension.

> ## Action Exercise
> Identify the persistent resentment issues building in your life right now and address them.
> *Are you carrying bitterness with you toward someone in your life?*
> *Are you angry, upset, or disappointed with your spouse or a friend over something they said or did? Something they didn't say or do?*

Pay attention the next time your anger flares up. Recognize the anger as something your body does to help you, and accept it. Take a deep breath. Then decide the most effective way to channel it and resolve the situation.

Resentment is very different from anger. Anger is a healthy emotion that occurs as an immediate reaction to something that just happened. Anger is generated quickly and can dissipate quickly if it is properly managed. Resentment, on the other hand, is a slow-burning bitterness that develops when we dwell on unresolved feelings of anger or betrayal. Anger is an emotion, but resentment is actually a choice we make. We have plenty of time to process our feelings as they build. We can choose to hold onto them for long periods of time or we can choose to let them go.

While anger can be channeled as a benefit, being resentful only leads to hurting ourselves. Carrying resentment is like drinking poison and expecting the other person to die. It is costly when it comes to those we care about, and downright stupid when it comes to those we don't. Allowing negative feelings to linger is the emotional equivalent of letting dishes pile up in the sink because we don't feel like doing the work required to clean them. Those feelings will continue growing until we deal with them. Or until they finally deal with us.

Resentment is the great destroyer of relationships, and most of the time it is preventable. Instead, we get upset and we sweep a little frustration under the bed without addressing it. We get angry and we sweep a little more. Over time we've accumulated a giant pile of crud and neither person can breathe anymore.

Little problems and misunderstandings can always be talked through. A growing heap of resentment will ruin marriages and friendships.

Given how valuable our relationships are to us, those important enough to be in our lives deserve our honesty and openness, our explanations and apologies. We all make mistakes, and we all feel the pressures of life. The people closest to us are the easiest targets. We have to be very careful not to project our own shortcomings and disappointments onto them. When teammates stop working together, the situation devolves into competition against each other. Eventually the growing resentment makes the situation intolerable. It is a malignant cancer that can only be prevented by addressing our issues with our friends and family members before it spreads too far. The sooner the better.

Resolving our issues with those we care about before they fester is almost always worth the time and effort required. But what is to be gained by harboring resentment toward those who aren't even a part of our lives? I am always amazed when a friend becomes visibly agitated discussing someone with whom they have very little interaction.

When we have the power to decide how others make us feel, why would we intentionally suffer for nothing? We cannot change the behavior of these people, nor should we care enough to want to. Yet, some of us still hold onto that resentment and hurt ourselves. The poet Sonya Teclai said, "Don't take anything personally from someone you're not personal with." The people outside our inner circle cannot have any effect on our happiness unless we allow them to. Let it go.

If the target of your resentment is not someone close to you, force yourself to let it go. If unresolved negativity is building between you and someone you care about, make it a point to talk it out. It may not be an immediate fix, but it might get the ship heading back in the right direction.

12

The Waste of Worrying

My philosophy is worrying means you suffer twice.

—J.K. ROWLING,
BRITISH AUTHOR

Like anger, worrying is natural and helpful up to a certain point, after which it begins to destabilize everything from our mental state to our productivity. Left unchecked, it will hinder our ability to function at a normal level, costing us time and wearing on our relationships. Worrying persists when we forget there are a limited number of variables we can influence. We must condition ourselves to be content handling only what we can control at this moment without wasting our time and energy on the things we cannot know in the future. As basketball legend Michael Jordan, a master of remaining focused in the present, put it, "Why would I think about missing a shot I haven't taken?" Each of us can instill that same disciplined mind-set, and we risk suffering serious consequences when we don't.

Excessive worrying is the result of our mistaken belief that we have more control than we actually do. When we embrace the inevitable uncertainties that constantly await all of us, we can live more calmly in the here and now. Otherwise, we will be relentlessly tormented by the unknown and the unknowable. Ironically, it is our fear of losing control that causes us to actually lose control. As the Roman philosopher Seneca said, "Many are harmed by fear itself, and many may have come to their fate while dreading fate." Once again, we do it to ourselves.

Stopping worry in its tracks can be made a habit. When we feel it coming on, we simply need to ask ourselves, "Am I content with the decisions I've made based on the knowledge I have right now?" That's it. If we have done our part, then we must allow events to unfold and await new information to act on. Preparing for different scenarios is wise. Frightening ourselves before anything changes is foolish. To paraphrase Michael Jordan, there is no logical reason or benefit to experience the negative effects of an outcome that hasn't taken place yet. It only wastes more of our valuable time.

Excessive worrying is not only mentally debilitating, but it takes a toll on our bodies as well. Thomas Jefferson was well aware of this connection back in 1816, when he wrote to John Adams, "...there are indeed (who might say Nay) gloomy and hypochondriac minds, inhabitants of diseased bodies, disgusted with the present, and despairing of the future; always counting that the worst will happen, because it may happen. To these I say How much pain have cost us the evils which have never happened!"

Worrying was once essential to human survival. There was a time when our lives were actually in danger every day, and our bodies were programmed with a stress response system to deal with those threats. "Today we may be living in high-rise apartments with overstuffed refrigerators, but our DNA still thinks we are in the savannah," Israeli historian Yuval Noah Harari asserts in *Sapiens*. We may no longer have to protect ourselves from wild animal attacks on our way back from lunch, but our brains haven't shed that functionality yet.

On the other hand, our primitive ancestors never had to juggle the added pressures of mortgages, careers, and college tuition. Our stress response system was designed to be activated only in an emergency in order to keep us alive; it was not designed to tolerate systemic abuse. In *Behave: The Biology of Humans at Our Best and Worst,* neuroendocrinology researcher Robert Sapolsky explains, "If you're stressed like a normal mammal in an acute physical crisis, the stress response is lifesaving. But if instead you chronically activate the stress response for reasons of psychological stress, your health suffers." In other words, our bodies are not equipped to handle the excessive and unnecessary worrying our minds put them through today.

Elevated stress levels raise blood pressure, suppress our immune system, and disrupt our cognitive functions. They damage our health and affect our relationships. When we agonize about things that haven't even happened yet, think about how much extra suffering we're putting ourselves through. And to what end? Panic clouds our thinking and acts like fog in a maze. We need to be comfortable making the best decisions we can with the information we have now and deal with the consequences once we know what they actually are.

Action Exercise

Identify the chronic worries in your life. It could be your career, someone you care about, or an upcoming life change. Wherever uncertainty may be creating stress for you, ask yourself the following questions:

Do I have all the information I can reasonably ascertain about this situation?

Have I made the best decision with the information I have?

Have I prepared myself as well as I can for the possible outcomes?

Will worrying help me to change the outcome in any way?

Use your journal for this exercise and you can revisit these scenarios after they've come to pass. This can be a powerful exercise to reinforce the habit of reducing unnecessary worrying.

Sixty percent of the time, it works every time.

—BRIAN FANTANA,
PLAYED BY ACTOR PAUL RUDD
IN *ANCHORMAN*

———————————

Here is another big reason we shouldn't waste time and energy worrying about potential future outcomes: We are notoriously horrible predictors of how we will actually feel when they do occur. Research has proven that the human brain does a lousy job estimating how we will feel about something that happens later. For example, once an event is put on the calendar, a picture begins forming in our minds. We can visualize what the location will look like, whom we will see, what they will be wearing, and what food and drinks will be served. Amazingly, we seem able to place ourselves in that future setting and somehow determine what kind of time we're going to have when we get there. We are so certain about how we are going to feel that we can confidently declare, "This is going to suck!" or "We're going to have a blast!"

The reason we are able to make these predictions is that our minds are always creating visualizations for us. When we look into the future, we don't see gaps and holes for events that haven't happened yet. What we see are the guesses our brains are constantly making for us, creatively filling in all the details we have no possible way of knowing. Not surprisingly, many of those details are inaccurate. And yet we form real emotions and opinions based on those unreliable visions. Imagining is what our imagination is for. But, as Daniel Gilbert explains in *Stumbling on Happiness,* the blunder occurs when you end up "unthinkingly treating what you imagined as though it were an accurate representation of the facts."

Regardless of how many times we've surprised ourselves on the car ride home by saying, "That was actually a lot of fun," we continue to make faulty predictions about future events. Reserving judgment until after we've actually had the experience saves us plenty of wasted time and energy spent worrying about it. We can only know how we feel about what is happening right now, which is precisely where we should be focusing our time and energy.

Action Exercise

Pick out a future event and write down your thoughts about it. Maybe it's an upcoming meeting, a party, a project, whatever. Predict what you expect to experience and how you think you will feel when you are there. Then, after it's over, review your notes and see whether your initial emotions were justified. Not only is it interesting to compare the results, but this exercise should also begin to alert you to the many ways our brains often jump to conclusions.

There will always be events in our lives we cannot control, and we cannot accurately predict how we will feel when they unfold. Once we've adequately prepared ourselves, we need to put it out of our minds until we receive additional information to consider. Until then, we should be focusing our time and attention on what is important to us today. There is nothing gained by obsessing about what might happen tomorrow.

13

Confidence Is the Key

The question isn't who is going to let me;
it's who is going to stop me.

—AYN RAND,
RUSSIAN-AMERICAN WRITER
AND PHILOSOPHER

No other single trait can match the powerful impact on a person's success and relationships as the appearance of confidence. Confidence shows that we are comfortable with ourselves, no matter what we are doing or who we are with. It's an attitude that says we understand the situation and we belong in it. We aren't intimidated by the presence of any person or the prospect of any challenge. Confidence is not to be confused with arrogance. Arrogance tends to push people away, while confidence pulls them closer to us. As the following story demonstrates, confidence can open plenty of doors for us—literally.

A few years ago, two young men in Melbourne decided to test the power of confidence at several different security entrances in an attempt to fool as many people as they could. The plan was to act like they had special clearance to enter and see who would believe them. The only props separating David and Sean from ordinary citizens were reflective vests and fake walkie-talkies they had purchased for just a few dollars from an office supply store. They relied on the common assumption that someone wearing a reflective vest and carrying a walkie talkie must have been authorized to do something legitimate.

Starting off easy, the pair first tested the ticket attendant at a movie theater. Without even stopping to explain, the men strolled right past and enjoyed a free film. Deciding to up the ante, next they went to the zoo, where they expected to encounter a bit more resistance. Fear kicked in, and they needed fifteen minutes just to calm their nerves outside the entrance. "It would not be an overstatement to say walking toward the ticket booth felt like getting off a boat on Normandy," David said. Neither believed they would succeed. They were wrong.

The two men didn't even raise a hint of suspicion as they entered the zoo, with Sean even saying "g'day" directly to the ticket clerk. In fact, the only times they were questioned at the zoo were when families came up to ask them about the zoo's hours of operation and directions to the monkeys! They capped off this incredible day by treating themselves to a free Coldplay concert. They were initially turned away at the arena, but the confidence they had built up all day enabled them to continue trying different entrances until they eventually succeeded in getting inside.

Listen, here's the thing: If you can't spot the sucker
in the first half hour at the table,
then you are the sucker.

—MIKE MCDERMOTT,
PLAYED BY ACTOR MATT DAMON
IN THE POKER MOVIE, *ROUNDERS*

Without condoning the illegality of their actions, we can learn a few lessons from our two Australian pranksters. To begin with, people, by nature, trust what they see. This illustrates the single greatest advantage any of us can cultivate for ourselves: When we look the part, we are the part. Without displaying any credentials at all, David and Sean were able to gain access to multiple places where they didn't belong, solely by the manner in which they carried themselves. Had they appeared nervous or hesitant, they very likely would have aroused suspicions. If they could so easily (and repeatedly) fool security personnel with their confidence, just imagine the effects we can have on all the people we encounter throughout our own lives.

One of the key phrases my wife, Stacey, has worked tirelessly to drill into our children's minds is "Perception is reality." Or, as executive coach Marshall Goldsmith says, "It's not about you. It's about what other people think of you." David and Sean spent the entire day granting themselves access to several venues by manipulating how others saw them. It cannot be overstated just how impactful the appearance of confidence is with respect to the opportunities we will have throughout our lives. Other people will make major decisions about us, and those decisions are heavily influenced by how successful they think we can become. We are always drawn to those individuals who appear to have it all figured out. That is what confidence looks like, and why it is so important to show it.

Malcolm Gladwell's *Blink* explores the concept of "thin-slicing," which is our tendency to make quick decisions based on limited information. We thin-slice by spotting patterns and applying our experience and intuition to reach instant conclusions. It's how our brains attempt to process more efficiently. As a result of thin-slicing, we are frequently assessed and rated based only on brief interactions, and often with lasting significance.

This is precisely why cultivating our self-awareness is so vital: in order to mentally step outside our body, walk our mind across the room, and see ourself the way others do.

If someone were watching you from a chair in the corner, how would they describe you? They cannot see inside your head, so what you show them is who you are. Perception is reality. Whenever we meet someone new, the ability to *appear* confident on the outside is even more valuable than actually *being* confident on the inside.

If you think winning at poker is all about getting the best cards, then why do the same players continue to win? Poker is the ideal microcosm of our interpersonal relationships. The unskilled players focus primarily on their own cards. They bet when they have a good hand and fold when they don't. It reminds me of the people who focus on the fear and nervousness in their heads. Those are the suckers. Conversely, the better players know how to win even when they aren't holding the best cards. They focus on what the body language and actions of the other players are saying. They are also keenly aware that they are always being watched themselves.

A skilled poker player can read the table and see when other players lack confidence in their hands. Even with weak cards, the skilled players can bluff their way to a win by representing strength, betting big, and forcing the other players to fold their cards. The secret to winning at poker is no different from our interactions with other people: We have to be able to show them what we want them to see.

Nobody understood this better than psychologist Maria Konnikova, who became a poker player in order to learn more about life. She didn't even know how many cards were in a deck when she started, but she soon became an international champion with over $300,000 in tournament winnings. Konnikova's major insight came from reading the brilliant polymath John von Neumann's

1944 book, *Theory of Games and Economic Behavior.* Von Neumann based his game theory on poker, which balances the same two opposing forces as life itself—chance and control. Like poker, he wrote, "Real life consists of bluffing, of little tactics of deception, of asking yourself what is the other man going to think I mean to do?" Konnikova grasped that she didn't need the best cards, the most experience, or natural talents to win at poker. Her advantage would be her mastery over what her opponents could and couldn't see.

One of the biggest hurdles Konnikova had to overcome was a very common phenomenon called the *imposter syndrome,* an overpowering fear that we don't belong and will be outed as a fraud. It happens when we mistakenly think we are unqualified, that other people know far more than we do. It can make us feel like phonies inside and wreck our confidence for no valid reason. Konnikova overcame the imposter syndrome by using her psychological training to her advantage. As she explains in *The Biggest Bluff: How I Learned to Pay Attention, Master Myself and Win,* "It's a process known as *embodied cognition:* embody the feeling you want to express, and your mind and body will often fall into alignment." In other words, she fooled herself into feeling confident by projecting it to others. By acting confident, she became confident. When we recognize the imposter syndrome coming on, we need to identify it for what it is, and then maintain our confident persona until it becomes reality.

There is a monumental difference between appearing confident and actually being a fraud. Even when we feel nervous or scared, we can convey to others that we're not rattled that we belong in this situation. Simply by remaining collected and not shrinking from the moment, we've assumed a position of leadership. However, maintaining control over our emotions and demeanor is not the same as pretending to be someone we're not. A fraud misrepresents their relationships, their knowledge, or their accomplishments. A confident person represents their belief in their ability to become successful. We cannot expect others to believe in us unless we are first able to demonstrate we believe in ourselves.

To observe the ideal representation of confidence, pay careful attention to the boxers before a fight. Most of the time you will see two fearless warriors betraying not the slightest hint of trepidation about the imminent battle. Mike Tyson, one of the most successful heavyweight champions the world has ever seen, perfected the prefight intimidation routine. With searing intensity, he stared right through his opponents and then viciously pounded them from the moment the bell rang. Many of Tyson's fights ended quickly with his opponents knocked out cold. How could anyone not quiver inside as they entered the ring to face him?

Eventually, we learned that Tyson's fierce and frightening persona was all a well-cultivated act taught to him by his legendary trainer, Cus D'Amato. This staged psychological intimidation routine provided a critical edge for Tyson who, it would shock many to later learn, was actually scared every time he entered the ring. "I felt the same fear in my first fight as I did in my last fight," he admitted, "It never goes away." Who could have imagined that the invincible Iron Mike Tyson was actually terrified before every fight? Both Maria Konnikova and Mike Tyson mastered the same technique of projecting confidence to their opponents, well before they felt it inside themselves.

Confidence is a vital component in building all of our relationships. There is no guarantee it will magically transform every situation into a winning one. But when we display a lack of confidence, we are certainly stacking the odds of success against ourselves. Why should we ever allow this to happen? Remember: We don't have to have all the answers to be confident. We just have to show we aren't afraid of what we don't know. We have to show we are up to the challenge, whatever it might be. Because we absolutely are.

Action Exercise

The next time you feel fear or self-doubt in the presence of others, step outside your body and pretend you're watching yourself from across the room.

Do you look calm and comfortable?

Are you making eye contact with people when you talk with them?

Are you smiling and relaxed or are you fidgety?

Make it a habit to appear comfortable in every situation and don't let any moment be too big for you. That is what confidence looks like.

14

Risking Rejection

Never let the fear of striking out keep you from playing the game.

—BABE RUTH,
AMERICAN BASEBALL LEGEND

The idea of rejection is scary, even traumatic for many people. Rejection and confidence are often intertwined, but there is a crucial difference: Where confidence has more to do with our attitude and demeanor, the risk of rejection carries us through to a specific action. David and Sean, the two Australians with the reflective vests, risked rejection when they tested the security entrances. They realized they faced serious potential consequences if they were denied, but they did not allow those fears to deter them. For most of us, however, the consequences of rejection are often just a polite no. Then why are we so afraid of being rejected? Why would we rather throw away opportunities than face the possibility of being told no? What exactly are we protecting ourselves from?

The author Jia Jiang tried to answer these questions by setting a goal to purposely get rejected for a hundred days in a row. His book *Rejection Proof* details a series of social experiments that continued pushing the envelope further and further until no request felt too ridiculous to make. He asked a donut shop to make his donut custom-shaped. Then he asked a flight attendant if he could make an announcement on the airplane's loudspeaker. Along his journey, he discovered a few invaluable insights:

- The anticipation of rejection is what scares us; the actual rejection isn't painful at all.

- *Avoiding* rejection ultimately hurts us a lot worse than being rejected.

- It is always amazing what people will agree to when we have the courage to ask.

We don't all need to perform a series of crazy stunts like Jiang in order to overcome our fear of rejection, but we do need to begin chipping away at our mental roadblocks. Avoiding rejection doesn't protect us from disappointment and pain. Avoiding rejection prevents us from true happiness.

When we were children, our annual doctor's appointment usually generated anxiety for most of us because we knew we were likely to have at least one needle stuck into us. Some adults still have this fear. Yet the actual shot or drawing of blood is not that painful at all. Rejection is the exact same, except that the needle we dread is heading for our ego. As a result, we become too scared to ask reasonable questions, to speak up, and to disagree. We are unable to take chances or make the right decisions. This unhealthy apprehension limits our growth and happiness, but it can be easily overcome. We must approach each rejection as a stoplight on the road to success. We can slowly condition ourselves by facing them one at a time. Bite by bite of the elephant.

After we overcome the fear of being told no, we can stop slamming the door in our own face. To fully understand how irrational this panic is, let's consider the worst-case scenarios when we make our pitch and fail.

Will the police come and arrest us? Will the person be so offended by our request that they scowl or insult us? Will they physically harm us or chase us away? Hardly. In the real world, where most of us live, they might say no or apologize for having to say no. We will have lost absolutely nothing. In fact, while being rejected, I've occasionally received helpful advice or guidance. So, believe it or not, a rejection can end up being a benefit!

On the other hand, they very well might say yes. As difficult as we find saying no to other people, it is every bit as difficult for other people to say no to us. This is especially true in a professional setting, where most employees are expected to solve problems and accommodate requests. Their default position is generally set to yes, and especially when caught off guard. They are motivated to give us what we're asking for and, if they can't, they will most likely offer a compromise. Either way, we come out ahead. We lose only when we chicken out.

If you are perfectly content with the life you have now, you may be okay with staying inside your comfort zone. However, many of us want to grow and develop, and we cannot do that without fighting through discomfort. It is in those moments when we feel most uneasy that we have the most to gain.

Imagine two serious-looking guards, posted in front of steel gates, staring intensely at you. What you want is just on the other side. As you approach the guards, and they turn their eyes to meet yours, you begin to doubt yourself. You tense up and your adrenaline kicks in. You begin to feel like you don't belong there. You feel like an imposter. You should probably turn back, right?

This is the very moment that crushes the spirit: standing at the threshold of something we want, seeing how close it is, and knowing we must ask if we want to get it. But solely to prevent the potential embarrassment of being denied, we foolishly let it all go. We completely misread the frightening guards, who aren't actually there to keep us out. They're looking for reasons to let us in. Confidence and willingness to face rejection is what opens the gates for us time and again. We won't always get inside, and we won't always get what we want when we do, but we should never take an opportunity away from ourselves.

---

*Sooner or later, those who win
are those who think they can.*

—PAUL TOURNIER,
SWISS AUTHOR

Job interviews are the quintessential "guard and gate" situations. There are nearly always several people competing for a limited number of available positions. We need to be comfortable with rejection if we are going to face those odds, and not allow ourselves to be demoralized or deterred when we aren't selected. The more we bring ourselves to those gates, the more opportunities we have for them to open for us.

Confidence and a willingness to risk rejection are the two essential attributes we must bring into the interview process. Combine those with a clear understanding of the actual point of the interview, and we give ourselves a much better shot against other candidates. I've interviewed many people over the years and participated in several hiring discussions. The entire interview process always revolves around a single question that is almost never actually asked. Regardless, the candidate who answers it best is most likely to be hired. The question is, "How can you make us better?"

That's really all there is to it. Most candidates are assumed to be qualified for the position, or they wouldn't have been included in the process. Some resumes might be more impressive than others, but we hire people, not paper. The job offers go to those who are able to project the kind of confidence that says, "You are a better company with me working here." To do that, we incorporate the concepts we've just learned. Our interviewers will thin-slice us, and we have a short window to show them who we are and why our experiences and abilities set us apart from the others. Projecting confidence and speaking proudly of what we've done are the attributes of a future leader, and every company wants to hire a leader.

Even when we perform perfectly, however, we aren't guaranteed a job offer. And if we are okay hearing the word no a few times, we will keep going until we get a yes. But if we cannot overcome our fear of being passed over, then we can pretty much give up on getting what we want out of life. Success rarely happens in a straight line. It usually takes zigging and zagging to get where you want to go.

Early in his career, Anderson Cooper's prestigious Yale education was somehow insufficient to land him a job at ABC answering phones and making copies. That rejection nudged him toward his current career as one of the most famous journalists in the world. "As it turned out, not getting that entry-level job there was the best thing that ever happened to me," Cooper said. A rejection often redirects us toward a better situation, which is another reason to accept it as a necessary step in the process.

It is also important to remember that an initial rejection isn't always a final decision. We never know what is happening in another person's mind, or whether we will eventually get another shot. Not only should we be comfortable being rejected, but we also need to maintain our confidence and composure when it happens to us. The way we handle the situation can actually turn the situation in our favor, as the following story will illustrate.

Our company had been interviewing candidates for a position, but we could not get unanimous agreement on a single person. One gentleman followed up with us and e-mailed a thoughtful presentation he had taken the time to put together. "I was thinking about your business needs from our discussion, and I put some ideas together," he wrote. "Hopefully, they might be helpful. I enjoyed meeting all of you." Not only were we all very impressed by this gesture, but we also decided to bring him back in for another interview, after which he was immediately hired. Sometimes the initial rejection is the first step in a sequence that ends exactly the way we want it to.

Finally, we should never squander the opportunity to learn something valuable from a rejection. Instead of just thanking someone for their time, ask for some advice. Two good question are:

- What do you recommend I improve on?
- What could I have done differently that might have helped?

Whether it is a kid cut from a sports team or an adult cut from the interview process, receiving that kind of feedback can be very helpful for next time. Of course, it can feel embarrassing and uncomfortable to continue a conversation with the people who just told us we aren't wanted. However, those with the confidence to ask these questions leave a positive impression that may pay off later on. More importantly, by asking for advice on how we can improve, we may walk out with the help we need to succeed. A rejection is never a waste of time when we can learn something from the experience.

Consider the level of rejection most stand-up comics have endured while bombing on stage. As Amy Schumer explains, "There's nothing louder than 5,000 people not laughing at you." When being funny is your job, there is a lot of pressure to deliver for the audience, and even more when you have to follow a disappointing performance. The way Schumer and other successful comics eventually found laughter was by continually facing that rejection and becoming more comfortable on stage. "It's not necessarily that the jokes get that much better," she explained, "you just own it more." The same principle applies to many other careers, particularly in sales. The more we face rejection, the more comfortable we become and the more our confidence builds. We see our results improve and we begin to branch out and grow.

Babe Ruth played more than two decades in the major leagues with a career batting average of .342. That means one of the greatest players in the history of baseball failed to get a hit in nearly two out of every three times at the plate! Even the best players risk rejection every time they step into the batter's box because they know most of the time they're going to be denied. They also know that swinging the bat is the only way to get a hit. That is exactly how we all need to approach rejection and become comfortable moving past it. Remember: Every no brings us closer to a yes.

There are endless possibilities that range from easy

Action Exercise

Like Jia Jiang, have fun conditioning yourself to become comfortable with rejection. There are many examples in his book, but you can come up with some of your own. Some of my ideas:

Ask a restaurant for a specific table that you've selected.

Ask a retail store whether the price is negotiable if you buy multiple items.

Ask a bakery if you can come pick up some extra items for free when they close.

Volunteer to make solicitation calls for a charitable organization.

to awkward. The idea is to encourage the other person to think about your request and come up with a valid explanation for why they can't accommodate it. Just by making them consider your ask, you've succeeded. If they say yes, it's a bonus! The more rejection you face, the less you'll be afraid, and the more you will improve your confidence. That is the real win here.

15

Our Beliefs: We Don't Know
What We Don't Know

*If anyone can prove and show to me that I think
and act in error, I will gladly change it—
for I see truth, by which no one has been harmed.
The one who is harmed is the one who abides in
deceit and ignorance.*

—MARCUS AURELIUS,
ROMAN EMPEROR AND PHILOSOPHER

The saying "ignorance is bliss" means we can actually be happier when we are unaware of certain things. In other words, what we don't know cannot hurt us. A harmless shark passing below us while we are surfing is a perfect example. We are undoubtedly happier without that knowledge. However, I have my own saying, "unawareness of ignorance is never bliss," which means we only hurt ourselves by not remaining open to the possibility we could be wrong. What we don't know can absolutely hurt us when we close ourselves off from learning it. Being wrong is how we learn and grow; the smartest minds in the world continue to welcome new information that may change their views. As we will see with the next story, nothing good ever happens by stubbornly clinging to certainty in the face of competing facts.

Given the inherent self-centeredness of human beings, it should surprise no one to learn we used to believe our planet was the center of the universe. According to what is referred to as the geocentric model, everything in space, including the sun, was thought to revolve around our beloved Earth. This established belief remained unchallenged for over a thousand years. In the year 1543, a Polish scientist named Nicolaus Copernicus dared to suggest that all the planets, including Earth, might actually orbit the sun instead. Copernicus died soon after, and his heliocentric model languished for another century when the Italian Galileo Galilei and his telescope validated it.

Galileo's proof of the heliocentric model effectively shattered the very composition of the universe held since the beginning of time. As a reward for his groundbreaking discovery, Galileo was placed on trial by the Vatican and forced to recant his findings under threat of torture. Why? Because this new information placed the Church in a supremely inconvenient position: It could not admit Galileo was right without acknowledging certain interpretations of the Bible had been wrong. Faith triumphed over fact and, sadly, one of the most essential scientific discoveries in the history of mankind was discredited and discarded. All of humanity was denied this truth as a result. Fans of Galileo would have to wait 350 years before he would be officially vindicated. Not until the year 1992, decades after human beings actually traveled into space, did the Vatican finally admit they were wrong.

And yet, there are still people walking around today who will argue the Earth is flat.

The reason beliefs are so powerful is because our very identities can become intertwined with them. When we take a stand for something, we make it part of who we are. It can make it very painful for us to let go or change course.

People have lost their lives in disputes over religion, politics, gang colors, and even sports teams. New facts become unwelcome intruders when they challenge the foundation of our thinking and threaten our way of living.

Copernicus's idea was breathtaking, for not only did he place the sun at the center of the solar system, but he also simultaneously reduced Earth to just another planet in its orbit. Even when Galileo proved the theory to be true, the Church was so dug into its position that it refused to change course. They feared their entire structure was vulnerable. The same thing happens to many of us when we refuse to consider contradictory information that challenges our own beliefs.

Christopher Columbus may have discovered the New World, but his close-mindedness cost him the naming rights. Attempting to find a new route from Spain to Asia, Columbus sailed west until he landed in the Bahamas. Believing he had reached Indonesia, rather than the Americas, he even called the people he encountered there "Indians." Columbus was convinced he already knew the makeup of the entire world, and therefore refused to consider the possibility he had actually discovered a new continent (which he had). A few years later, Amerigo Vespucci made multiple voyages to the actual land Columbus found, but the open-minded Vespucci determined it was, in fact, a new continent. A mapmaker named Martin Waldseemüller credited Vespucci with discovering the New World, naming it America after him. Had Columbus been willing to question his own knowledge and beliefs, this book might have been published in the United States of Columbia.

Vespucci, Copernicus, and Galileo were able to see the world differently because they were *willing* to see it differently. This flexibility of mind exists in each of us, but to exercise it we must loosen our grip on our current knowledge and be open to receiving new information. It is impossible to learn we have been wrong when we have thoroughly convinced ourselves we are right. The Greek philosopher Aristotle said, "It is the mark of an educated mind to be able to entertain a thought without accepting it." Put another way, we should always listen to new ideas and test them against what we currently believe. Wisdom and knowledge are achieved only through a willingness to question everything. We don't know what we don't know.

Stubbornly entrenching ourselves in questionable or faulty beliefs stifles our learning and progress. It took over three centuries for the Catholic Church to finally admit they were wrong about Galileo. While it may be an extreme example, it does reveal the incredible determination some individuals will muster in clinging to an incorrect position. As Kathryn Schulz explains in *Being Wrong: Adventures in the Margin of Error,* people become deeply entrenched in their beliefs, driven by powerfully strong emotions. This creates giant blind spots in our thinking because "by definition, there can't be any particular feeling associated with simply being wrong. Indeed, the whole reason it's possible to be wrong is that, while it is happening, you are oblivious to it." Nobody ever says, "I'll bet you I'm wrong."

Again, we don't know what we don't know. But we sure put a lot more conviction into what we think we *do* know. The problem is, if it is impossible for us to actually *feel* wrong, how can we completely trust it when we *feel* right? The Earth does feel flat to all of us when we go for a walk, and that feeling becomes too powerful for a minority of people to let go. Their convictions are further bolstered by other members of Flat Earth societies all over the globe, none of whom I presume has ever seriously considered the international flight paths required to attend a Flat Earth convention. Like Galileo's discovery, those would be unwelcome facts threatening the foundation of their beliefs, so they ignore or discredit them. This is happening all around us.

By keeping our minds open to hearing opposing views, we don't miss out on those fortunate opportunities to improve our thinking. Instead of feeling attacked by those who disagree, why not be grateful to them for allowing us to test our knowledge basis? I appreciate the opportunity to discard a mistaken belief rather than continuing to carry it around with me. As John Maynard Keynes reportedly asked, "When the facts change, I change my mind. What do you do, sir?"

When you judge another, you do not define them.
You define yourself.

—WAYNE DYER,
AMERICAN AUTHOR AND SPEAKER

Being wrong is already a difficult thing for many people to concede, even when the facts are against them. After all, many accepted facts have been proven incorrect over time. Consider, then, those disputes where there are no established facts for either side of the argument. Generally, these disagreements concern a person's beliefs or preferences for which there is no correct answer. And yet, oftentimes they become heated and personal nonetheless.

Did God create man, or did man create God? Which religion does God want us to practice? Are there multiple gods? Is there a god at all? What is the most important painting in the Uffizi? Was Elvis Presley more influential than the Beatles? Was Michael Jordan a greater basketball player than LeBron James? You might feel very confident answering one or more of these questions, and quite capable of defending your reasoning. Unfortunately, there is no way to prove whether you are right or wrong.

Topics such as these are endlessly debated, but never fully settled. Each of us is on our own journey and our thinking will hopefully continue to evolve. We don't all see things the same way, and that's a very good thing. After all, we can't learn much if we spend all our time with people who think exactly like us. If we want to have more meaningful relationships in our lives, we need to welcome different perspectives and viewpoints.

When we challenge or minimize someone's beliefs or preferences, we not only offend them but we make ourselves look foolish and small. Sometimes we do this without even realizing it, by making sweeping generalizations. Consider the No True Scotsman fallacy, for example. As Kathryn Schulz explains it, "Let's say you believe that no Scotsman puts sugar in his porridge. I protest that my uncle, Angus McGregor of Glasgow, puts sugar in his porridge every day. 'Aye,' you reply, 'but no *true* Scotsman puts sugar in his porridge.'" This illustrates the danger of seeing the world only in black and white, when there are many shades of gray.

You may have a peculiar taste in porridge or irrational ideas about Scotsmen. Either way, you've just insulted my uncle Angus and irritated me with no benefit to yourself. Rather than waste our time, aggravate ourselves, and endanger our relationships, we can simply make room for another person's views. There have always been multiple political parties, religions, and genres of art. Keep that in mind the next time you're prepared to insult someone for seeing the world a little differently. By being respectful and tolerant of others, we can all order different entrees and still enjoy our dinner together at the same table.

Better to remain silent and be thought a fool than to speak and remove all doubt.

—ABRAHAM LINCOLN,
SIXTEENTH PRESIDENT
OF THE UNITED STATES

Being open to receiving new information is how we are able to improve our thinking and change our mind. The ability to learn and challenge our knowledge is one of the most valuable skills we can develop, and one of the most appreciated by others. Admitting wrongness is a sign of intelligence, not stupidity. It is an opportunity to show leadership, not weakness. Contrary to popular belief, leaders are not always expected to have the answers. True leaders are confident saying, "I don't know," "I need to think more about it," or "I need to gather more information before I can offer a reasoned opinion." Because a fool is afraid of appearing uninformed, they guess or make up an answer, which ironically destroys their future credibility. Every salesperson and customer service representative I have worked with memorized this sentence: "I don't have the answer, but I can get it for you soon." People will appreciate your honesty, but they will punish you for your bullshit.

Albert Einstein said, "I do not like to state an opinion on a matter unless I know the precise facts." Still, as Carlo Rovelli reminds us, "Einstein changed his mind many times on fundamental questions, and it is possible to find numerous erroneous phrases of his that contradict each other." Einstein wasn't always right, even though he was determined to speak only when he felt certain. His brilliance only grew because he consistently accepted being wrong and changed course accordingly. If perhaps the smartest person to ever live was comfortable changing his mind, how foolish are we to not follow suit? Remember, nobody likes being around a stubborn know-it-all. Winning an argument is seldom worth damaging a valuable relationship. The better we understand ourselves and the way we think, the more we can improve the relationships in our lives. It begins with our perspective and the way we see the world around us.

Action Exercise

Approach each argument as an opportunity to learn something.

Be on alert the next time you are engaged in a debate. If there are no conclusive facts that support either side, force yourself to respect another point of view and ask questions to understand the other person's reasoning better. Remain calm, test your own beliefs against theirs, and be willing to change your mind. In the end, it is often best to agree to disagree and move on.

When we control our anger, stop our growing resentments, and minimize unnecessary worrying, we can live in the present and make the most of our precious time. Having the confidence to be who we want to be and the willingness to risk rejection along the way is the only way to put ourselves on the right path. Finally, wisdom and knowledge come from a willingness to be wrong and to welcome new ideas and insights. Once we have instilled this foundation in ourselves, we will then be able to reap even more benefits from the other major relationships in our lives, beginning with our networks.

16

Our Networks

He that walketh with wise men shall be wise;
but a companion of fools shall be destroyed.

—SOLOMON,
PROVERBS 13:20

Every one of our relationships occupies a position in our network. This includes acquaintances, friends, colleagues, advisors, teammates and anyone else we spend time interacting with. Our network of relationships is part of the three things that matter most to us, and it must be regularly prioritized. Not everyone deserves to occupy a spot in our network, and we often have to make adjustments to allow room for those who do. We may feel like we know a lot of people, but the reality is there are a limited number of relationships we can maintain at one time.

Social media and technology advancements have made the process of communicating easier than ever before. Everyone is just a keystroke or swipe away. This often traps us into thinking our network is bigger than it actually is. The British anthropologist Robin Dunbar estimated the human brain is capable of comfortably maintaining a maximum of 150 stable relationships. He explained this as "the number of people you would not feel embarrassed about joining uninvited for a drink if you happened to bump into them in a bar." Beyond that point, our cognitive ability to recognize another person, remember their background, preferences, and associations is constrained. The majority of people we connect with will be through surface-level interactions.

In addition to our mental limitations, we simply have a finite amount of time we can invest in our network. Given the importance of both time and relationships to our lives, the opportunity costs can be expensive. When we spend our time on people who don't add value or enrich our experiences today, we also limit our possibilities for tomorrow. On the other hand, when we invest our time in the right people, we not only benefit from our own relationships, but from the network of relationships those people have built as well. This is why choosing individuals who also make good choices about others creates exponential gains for ourselves. Our time should be spent on those who appreciate us and improve our lives at the same time. So much of our happiness and success in life is a direct result of the quality of our relationships and our ability to manage them.

Friends and Acquaintances

Be careful who you call your friends.
I'd rather have four quarters than 100 pennies.

—AL CAPONE,
AMERICAN GANGSTER
AND BUSINESSMAN

If I ask you to draw a line down the center of a sheet of paper, then list your friends on the left side and your acquaintances on the right side, would you be able to do it? The majority of our relationships can be grouped into these two main categories and yet, too often we mistakenly blur the line between the two.

We err when we inadvertently take a friend for granted or place too much trust or reliance upon an acquaintance. Each person in our lives holds a different value and purpose for us, and we need to know which category they are in so we can actively manage our time among them.

There is a short exchange near the end of the movie *Tombstone* that beautifully exemplifies the meaning of friendship. Doc Holliday (played by actor Val Kilmer) is bedridden with tuberculosis as his friend Wyatt Earp sets off on a dangerous mission to bring the Clanton gang to justice. Knowing Wyatt is headed for trouble against the dreaded gunfighter Johnny Ringo, Doc sneaks out of his bed, finds Ringo, and outdraws him, thus saving Wyatt from serious danger. Shortly before this duel, the visibly ill Doc is shown rising from a rest under a tree, sweating and coughing near Turkey Creek Jack Johnson (played by actor Buck Taylor).

Jack: Doc, you ought to be in bed, what the hell you doin' this for anyway?

Doc: Wyatt Earp is my friend.

Jack: Hell, I've got lots of friends.

Doc: I don't.

Every time I watch the movie with my sons, I pause it after this scene and make sure they understand exactly what it means. In just two words, Doc Holliday cuts right through the difference between friends and acquaintances. The Earps are Doc's friends and there wasn't even a second thought given to being there for them. Turkey Creek Jack Johnson, on the other hand, has only *acquaintances*. If he had real friends, he would have understood why Doc was there.

Friends are vital to our self-esteem, provide us with support and inspiration, and are responsible for many incredible shared experiences. In addition to enjoying leisure activities together, friends are reliable and available in times of need. Friendships, both old and new, require regular voluntary investments of time to build and maintain. Just spending time together, as teammates or coworkers for example, isn't enough. Two people *choosing* to spend quality time together is what real friendships are built on.

University of Kansas professor Jeffrey Hall is a nationally recognized expert on relationships. In 2018, he published the results of a study on the time investments required for friendships to be formed. Here is what he discovered:

- Casual friendships emerge when forty to sixty hours are spent together within the first six weeks of meeting.

- Casual friends may transition to friends after about eighty to 100 hours spent together.

- Good or best friends don't emerge until after 200 hours are spent together.

According to the study, it requires an average of seven hours a week for six weeks to become casual friends. Making the jump to friends and then good/best friends requires far more quality time together. Unless we are actively building deeper connections outside a school or work environment, these are considered situational friendships, which belong in the same category as acquaintances. They generally fade over time when those situations change.

What determines the depth of a relationship is the amount of time we choose to spend with each other outside of our closed systems. Investing our most valuable asset—time—in any person creates another valuable asset—a relationship. How valuable that asset becomes depends on the amount of time spent and the quality of the person we spend it on.

Friends have been invited into each other's homes and have met spouses or other family members. They get together in the evenings and on the weekends. Friends check in with each other just to say hello and catch up. They remember important events and perform selfless acts of generosity. Friends show up in times of need without having to be asked. Friends care enough about each other to volunteer honest and undiluted feedback, regardless of how uncomfortable it may be. When a reality check is necessary, friends are willing to probe our delusions and help us clear the pathway for self-awareness and growth.

Acquaintances, according to Hall's study, rarely choose to spend more than thirty hours together over a nine-week period. Acquaintances occupy less prestigious positions in our network but still serve important personal and professional roles. They may not be part of our inner circle but they will be welcome friendly companions on certain occasions. They may provide us with information, assistance, or entertainment, and may often serve as valuable links to other people and opportunities. For these reasons, we should always take the opportunity to meet new people and keep in touch when it is practical. However, we must be careful not to prioritize them over our friends.

Managing our relationships is a balancing act, and there are always opportunity costs. It is nearly impossible to maintain several close friendships and a robust group of acquaintances. Those who attempt this end up spreading themselves too thin, depleting the quality of their friendships and the depth of those connections. Remember Doc Holliday and Turkey Creek Jack Johnson. I reserve the term "friend" for a select few people, and it saddens me to see those who miss out on these truly special and rare relationships because they were unable to prioritize their time or make the necessary commitments. Would you rather spend less time with several different people you aren't particularly close with, or spend more time with the few people with whom you've shared many special occasions and deep conversations?

Over time, we must constantly reprioritize and reevaluate our friends and acquaintances. This includes setting boundaries, minimizing and even eliminating time spent with certain individuals. People evolve and relationships do as well. Not everyone is meant to become a friend and not every friendship is meant to last forever. Proximity also plays an important role in our relationships, as I discovered when I moved from Chicago to Omaha. Some of my oldest and closest friends are still part of my network, though we do not interact on a regular basis. Technology can be helpful, but it will never substitute for the magic of time spent in another's presence.

Our networks may be capable of supporting up to 150 people, but research indicates we have frequent contact with only around fifteen of them. These are the friends and acquaintances with the most influence over our daily lives. The quality of these relationships depends largely on how effective we are at approaching, building, and managing them. Next, we take a deeper dive into understanding and improving those processes.

How Relationships Thrive or Die

You can't stay in your corner of the Forest waiting for others to come to you. You have to go to them sometimes.

—WINNIE THE POOH,
A.A. MILNE

Given how important relationships are to us, it's a wonder how often we sabotage our opportunities to have them. When it comes to meeting new people, many of us are split into two camps: either we cannot summon the interest or energy to do it, or we lack the social skills to do it properly. Both groups are making huge mistakes. As Hall's research teaches us, the first several weeks after an initial meeting often determine the kind of relationship two people will have, or whether there will be one at all. Mishandling these early interactions drastically limits or delays the potential benefits of these associations, with detrimental, long-lasting ramifications.

Thanks to the technology revolution, it has never been easier to connect, interact, share, and communicate with people across the entire globe. We were promised a world in which these tools would bring us closer together than our parents' generation. And yet, despite all our modern conveniences, we are experiencing a global epidemic of loneliness. A 2018 study by the Kaiser Family Foundation found that 22 percent of adults in the United States and the United Kingdom say they often feel lonely, lack companionship, or feel isolated. The majority of these people are under fifty years old. More than one in every five of us is experiencing an erosion in the quality of our relationships, impairing our physical and mental well-being.

For the past several years, human progress has been marked by innovative new ways to pack our lives ever more tightly with activities and distractions. Because our time is so precious, we have pursued ways to do as many things as we can. As a result of this culture shift toward doing more and more, a great paradox has emerged: We have devalued each moment and normalized the constant hurrying from one obligation to the next. Our minds are often everywhere else except where they should be focused—right here in the present. We rob ourselves of the simple pleasures of a moment by not being fully engaged. We have shortened our attention spans, disrupting the actual process of meeting new people and exploring substantive or meaningful conversations. We are often too distracted or disinterested at any particular moment to welcome another person into our busy lives.

Close relationships are vital to our well-being, and as we've recently struggled to form new ones, an ominous trend toward loneliness has developed.

One particular experience taught me how naïve and costly it can be to believe we don't need to meet new people. Several years ago, I brought my oldest son Zach to a kindergarten birthday party at a miniature golf course. We arrived around the same time as Zach's new friend Chase and his dad. The boys ran off together, and the dad introduced himself to me. In the past, I would have typically been polite, made small talk, and found a way to get out of there. Partly because I was excited Zach had made a new friend at a new school, and partly because Scott (the dad) was so friendly and engaging with me, I ended up staying and talking with him for the rest of the party. That decision launched one of the great friendships of my life.

There is no question Scott and I would have run into each other many times again, due to our boys' friendship. However, as Professor Hall's study on forming friendships revealed, our relationship would have taken a very different route. We wouldn't have spent the next several weeks getting to know each other over lunches and cocktails. From our first conversation, we discovered mutual interests and similar senses of humor. We have multiple kids the same ages, and we bonded over youth sports. Not only have Zach and Chase maintained a special friendship for over a decade, but our entire families have as well. We have celebrated many special events, holidays, and vacations together. It is difficult for me to imagine not having them in our lives. And yet, without that initial conversation with Scott, most of it likely would never have happened.

Surrounding ourselves with the best people has invaluable benefits. One of the many ways Scott's friendship has improved my life has been his impact on my interactions with other people. Where I was naturally less comfortable meeting new people and making small talk, he would willingly engage other people in the room. I learned he was no social butterfly, and he, too, placed a premium on prioritizing his time among friends and acquaintances. Unlike me, Scott motivated himself to talk with people in social situations and not waste easy opportunities to explore potential new connections. Once it hit me that this was precisely what he'd done with me at the birthday party when we first met, the lightbulb went on in my head. This was a huge insight, and it changed the way I would approach every future encounter.

Every relationship requires both a willingness and an effort made to meet another person. While we cannot realistically swap stories with everyone we randomly bump into, we would be unwise not to engage someone we share an existing connection with. This includes friends of friends, neighbors, parents of our children's friends, guests at parties and work functions, and people we keep running into. While it may seem more comfortable to avoid these seemingly trivial interactions, there are huge hidden costs in doing so. Anyone can end up playing a significant role in our lives and we don't always know who, how, or when. What we know for certain is every time we choose not to engage with another person we close ourselves off from a potentially valuable relationship.

Everything flows once we break the ice. It took a little work, but I conditioned myself to no longer rely on the other person to do it. Once again, self-confidence and the willingness to be rejected are vital tools in developing the ability to approach and talk with people we don't know. Carrying a conversation may feel uncomfortable at times, but like anything else, our social skills only improve with practice. It might feel awkward in the beginning, but it is far less awkward than dodging people and avoiding eye contact. Our relationships are one of the three things that matter most, and they can happen only when two people talk with each other. If this remains a challenge for you, then improving your communication skills should be one of your highest priorities.

First Impressions

> *You never get a second chance to make a first impression.*
>
> —WILL ROGERS,
> AMERICAN ACTOR AND HUMORIST

The reason more deserving individuals often get shafted is because most major decisions about people aren't made on fairness. They're made on feeling. They are also made fairly quickly and, once made, are not easily changed. This is the thin-slicing Malcolm Gladwell wrote about in *Blink.* First impressions are always thin-sliced; people have already formed a concrete impression of us well before they've gotten to know our character or abilities. These snap evaluations, based on limited information and brief interactions, can stick for a long time. A strong first impression today can pay huge dividends in your personal or professional life in the future, while a poor first impression can cost you in ways you may never realize.

In the summer before entering high school, I began practicing with the freshman football team. Nearly all the kids on the team were strangers to me. An odd dichotomy existed in that we were all competing with each other for positions on the team, yet at the same time evaluating each other as potential friends. There was one kid on the team I did not hit it off with at all. We reverted to our primal selves, trying to intimidate each other like two male lions battling for control of the pride. We even looked alike.

After a couple of weeks, the other boy and I sat near each other on the steps just before practice. He looked down at my feet, then through a sideways glare said, "Nice cleats." That's all it took, and the ice was broken between us. Rich told that story as a groomsman at my wedding eleven years later about how we met. He's been one of the most important people in my life ever since, and it's amazing given how badly we both botched our first impressions with each other. I can only imagine how many potential relationships I torpedoed over the years by my own stupidity.

We have two ears and one tongue so that we would listen more and talk less.

—DIOGENES,
GREEK PHILOSOPHER

Developing interpersonal skills is far more important to us than whatever our technical skills may be. The earlier in life we discover this, the more opportunities we create for ourselves. I constantly stress this to my children, because there are still some adults who haven't figured it out yet. Doors are always opening and closing for us based solely on our brief interactions with other people. There's a reason nobody focuses on second impressions. We don't always get the opportunity to make them. Once I realized how badly I had been blowing it for so long, I committed to getting it right. I developed my own four-part game plan for making a strong first impression, using the mnemonic CLIP:

- project *confidence*
- *listen*
- be *interested*
- *positive* close

Putting this framework in place calmed my nerves and grew my comfort level with having conversations. Before long, it actually began feeling natural to me. The best part about CLIP is it continues to be useful with every relationship we have, not just the new ones.

CLIP begins with the key to most of our successes: *confidence*. As we have already seen, our brains continue to function in many ways the same as they did for our ancient ancestors. As a result, we immediately evaluate someone new as a threat or an ally. Are they nice or mean? Are they strong or weak? Am I safe or in danger? We thin-slice instantaneous judgments based on the way people carry themselves, and they do the same with us. Confidence is attractive to us. Nervousness signals weakness. Confident people make eye contact and smile. Nervous people look away or hide on their phones. Confident people take control and lead the exchange. Nervous people wait uncomfortably to see if the other person will say something. Perception is reality. What you show other people is what you are. When in doubt, be proud of who you are and remind yourself people are lucky to meet you. That's what confidence feels like.

The second part of CLIP is to listen. Listening is not just politely waiting for our turn to talk. A conversation is a discussion, not a presentation. When we listen, we relax our urge to speak and allow the other person's words to sink in. Too often we treat conversations like movie scenes, where our dialogue is prepared in advance. This works well for performances and speeches, but it fails miserably for personal interactions.

I used to prepare my responses while other people were talking so I would have something interesting to say when it was my turn to speak. Unfortunately, whenever the conversation had shifted, my well-crafted and thoughtful responses were no longer timely or relevant. I couldn't keep up with the discussion. Since I started actively listening, it has become much easier to follow up on interesting points, discover things I have in common with others, and spot those perfect cues for me to share information.

It's important to remember we don't have to know all the answers, and we don't need a witty or intelligent remark ready to share. A conversation is like an unchoreographed dance between people and should flow naturally between them. When we aren't listening, it's like clumsily dancing by ourselves.

Actively listening also enables us to demonstrate *interest* in the other person, which is the third part of CLIP. The legendary Dale Carnegie, author of *How to Win Friends and Influence People,* said, "You can make more friends in two months by being interested in other people than you can in two years by trying to get other people interested in you."

With that in mind, here is one of the most valuable tricks I can teach you: The more you get people to talk, the more they will like you afterward. Studies provide two crucial findings for why this works: Talking about ourself triggers the same pleasure sensation in the brain as eating delicious food, and people who ask more questions in a conversation are liked better by those who talked with them. To accomplish both, we keep the other person talking by asking open-ended questions, which don't have simple yes or no answers. For example, "What do you think about…" or "How did you meet…" When we do this, we can't help but leave a positive impression.

It seems counterintuitive, but simply by resisting the urge to share more, we actually become more interesting to others. The challenge lies in overcoming a deeply ingrained (and deeply wrong) belief that we need to impress other people for them to like us. Like some kind of audition, we throw it all out there, selling ourselves, dominating the conversation, and ultimately ending up boring the other person. When in doubt, always err on the side of modesty. Truly great individuals don't need to broadcast their own accomplishments or justify their importance. It is the hallmark of an insecure person to drop names and flaunt associations in an effort to boost their own status. My sister-in-law, Carin, likes to say, "It only means something to me when someone else drops *your* name." I love her attitude and it is the exact mind-set we want to cultivate—let others tell your story.

Pay attention to the great interviewers, and the way they maintain focus on their guests with minimal interjections about themselves. They ask open-ended questions to keep the guest talking. For example, "Tell me more about that," or "What was that like?" Likewise, we should answer questions briefly and thoughtfully, remembering to steer the conversation back to the other person.

Not only will they get to talk more about themselves, but we will also get to learn more about their beliefs, interests, and values. This allows us to better understand areas of commonality and areas of disagreement, all without inadvertently irritating or offending them. We are like onions with many layers and when we peel them off too quickly there is no mystery left. It never hurts to under-share. Not only will the other person like us more for listening to them talk but they will also be motivated to get to know us better. As they say in the theater: Always leave them wanting more.

The final piece of the CLIP is a *positive close,* which puts the finishing touch on the impression we leave. The end of our interaction with someone carries a lot of weight, as Larry David demonstrated with "The Big Good-bye" in his show *Curb Your Enthusiasm.* After deliberately ignoring a person all evening at a party, Larry would deliver a brief but exuberant good-bye just before exiting. This positive close left the person feeling special despite being largely avoided. Although utilized as a purely comedic vehicle for the show, the maneuver is rooted in psychological reality.

Consider the effect a bad ending to a movie or song can have on the overall experience. Keep that in mind when you close a conversation. It generally sets the tone for how you will be remembered. Whether our time has run out, or the discussion has stalled, it is perfectly appropriate to make a graceful exit. Something as simple as "It was nice talking with you" will work, but I always try leave the impression that this was only the beginning of a longer conversation. Some examples include:

- It was really great talking with you, let's do it again sometime soon.
- I'm sorry that I have to be somewhere. I would have enjoyed talking more.
- I'd like to stay and talk with you more, but I should probably go say hello to a couple of people. Let's plan to continue this conversation.

In each of these examples, we are keeping the door open to welcome a future interaction. We aren't leaving them feeling cut off or cast aside for someone more interesting. Also, avoid being caught up in the moment and making empty promises. People remember them. When someone says "Let's get together and have lunch" or "Let's grab a drink" but never follows through, it does more harm than good. Even when we throw out an unspecific invitation, we should plan to follow up in the next few days. Honoring commitments reflects upon the quality of our character.

If we want the opportunity to build meaningful relationships, we have to become proficient at making first impressions. We should be confident, actively listen, demonstrate interest, and close positively. That's all there is to it. Stick to the CLIP, and it is hard to mess it up.

The Right Way to Build Relationships

> *If you go looking for a friend, you're going to find they're very scarce. If you go out to be a friend, you'll find them everywhere.*

—ZIG ZIGLAR,
AMERICAN SALESMAN
AND MOTIVATIONAL SPEAKER

> **Action Exercise**
>
> Practice working the CLIP method into your conversations with people you already know until you get comfortable actively listening and demonstrating interest. Then build your confidence by trying it on someone new.
>
> Really focus on the other person's words until you are comfortable not planning out your responses in advance. Allow them to finish their sentences without jumping in too quickly. Practice keeping the conversations moving with open-ended questions.

The process of building relationships is like growing a garden. We cannot make the obvious mistake of approaching every relationship the same way. First we determine whether a new flower or shrub is a good fit and what kind of role it will have. Then we plant it by identifying key interests and making connections. Next we water it by following up on those interests and connections.

Just as every plant has different preferences and needs, so does every person. Water a plant too much or too often, and you'll drown it. Don't water it enough, and it wilts and fades. It may end up taking over too much space and need to be trimmed back. The same goes for relationships. With the right arrangement and the appropriate balance, they will bloom over time.

Whether the potential connection is personal or professional, once we've determined someone new is worth making room for in our lives, we want to give the relationship every opportunity to succeed. The strongest relationships are the product of three key motivations:

- thoughtfulness
- generosity
- genuineness

No relationship will advance beyond the initial stage without all of them.

It all begins with thoughtfulness, which is a desire to show someone we care. While we are actively listening to them, we should be scanning for clues about things with real meaning to them. What would they want to do or receive as a gift for their birthday? Are there specific things they prefer to eat or drink, activities they enjoy, teams or artists they are passionate about? Take mental notes when things stand out, and later type them into a contact card or write them in your journal.

Demonstrating thoughtfulness is as simple as showing a person we made an effort to remember something. I might follow up with them by calling, texting, or e-mailing something I feel they might appreciate. If I come across an article or a review about something they mentioned, I will forward them the link. If I hear of an upcoming event that might interest them, I will share it. "Hey, I just heard Pearl Jam is coming to town next month." I might ask, "Will I see you there?" Thoughtfulness is about finding common ground and building connections.

Generosity is taking our thoughtfulness and putting it into action. It could be picking up the check for lunch or drinks. It could be buying tickets to a concert. It could be a gift T-shirt or a hat. It doesn't have to be expensive, and it should never go overboard, but it should be a selfless gesture with no strings attached. For example, I have built some wonderful relationships over the years throughout the bourbon community. As a result, I have been fortunate to gain access to many rare and special bottles. This has allowed me to give some pretty special gifts to people when I know it would mean a lot to them. Each of us can find something meaningful to benefit another person when we combine thoughtfulness and generosity.

In *Influence: The Psychology of Persuasion,* Robert Cialdini describes what he calls the *rule of reciprocity,* whereby people are inherently motivated to return a favor done for them. We learn this behavior from a young age, and it subconsciously influences many of our interactions. Doing something generous for someone else creates a feeling of obligation toward us. This is often exploited as a sneaky trick; for example, when gifts or samples are offered in an effort to motivate purchases. However, this innate desire to reciprocate can be quite effective in building relationships, provided our motivations are genuine.

"A growing relationship can only be nurtured by genuineness," author and speaker Leo Buscaglia astutely noted. Meaningful relationships should never be transactional. We need to accept the people in our lives for who they are, how they treat us, and how they make us feel. The surest way to spoil a relationship is to keep score or place strings on thoughtful gestures. We should naturally return the kindness when we can, but never let the rule of reciprocity get in our heads and create awkwardness. Once we allow expectations of one person owing the other to fester, it can devalue the essence of the relationship and lead to hurt feelings.

Building relationships requires us to invest our precious time, combining two of the three things that matter most. We build our best relationships when we are thoughtful with our listening, generous in our actions, and genuine in our intentions. We will not always be successful in our efforts with these three motivations, but we are doomed to certain failure without them.

Character: You Never Know Who Is Watching

The true test of a man's character is what he does when no one is watching.

—JOHN WOODEN,
BASKETBALL COACH

The superstars of every sport all agree that exhibitions never existed for them. They competed the exact same way whether in practice or in a packed arena. There wasn't an on/off switch to flip or a time to give less than a full effort. We need to bring that same mentality to all of our interpersonal interactions, regardless of who is there or what the stakes appear to be. We cannot just wait to "turn it on" when important people are around or when we think it matters. It *always* matters.

The reality is we never know who is watching, or what it might eventually mean for us. In Patrick Lencioni's *The Ideal Team Player,* Ted Marchbanks was the leading candidate for a major management role at Valley Builders. Ted had been successful enough to retire from his career with a competitor, and his glowing reputation preceded his interview at Valley Builders. He had everything working in his favor and the interview appeared to be little more than a formality. Valley Builders desperately needed someone with Ted's qualifications and experience. What could possibly go wrong?

Ted may have seemed like he'd be a perfect fit, but he just didn't know who was watching him at Valley Builders. The receptionist, Kim, escorted Ted to his various interviews throughout the day, but he didn't even bother to remember her name. He never considered the possibility that Kim the receptionist would be asked by the company's key decision makers to provide her opinion of Ted that afternoon. Kim would share with her bosses that she and Ted spent fifteen minutes in the lobby together than morning and he didn't bother to ask her a single question. She would reveal that over the course of a few hours, the only two times Ted actually spoke to her were when he needed directions to the bathroom and to find a place to charge his phone. Ted felt he was too important to waste his energy on someone beneath his level, and this red flag on his character cost him the job. *Remember:* You never know who is watching.

Perhaps no movie character better personifies our misconceptions about other people than the janitor Carl Reed, played by actor John Kapelos in *The Breakfast Club.* While cleaning the room during a Saturday detention, Carl is mocked by smart-aleck student John Bender, played by actor Judd Nelson. "How does one become a janitor?" Bender condescendingly asks Carl, "Because Andrew here is very interested in pursuing a career in the custodial arts." Instead of being angry or upset at the belittling, Carl proudly fires back this splendid response:

You guys think I'm just some untouchable peasant? A serf? Peon? Maybe so. But following a broom around after shitheads like you for the last eight years I've learned a couple of things. I look through your letters. I look through your lockers. I listen to your conversations. You don't know that, but I do. I am the eyes and ears of this institution, my friends. By the way, that clock's twenty minutes fast.

As Carl calmly exits, Bender's smile reveals how poorly he had misjudged the situation. People often aren't who you assume they are. Later in the movie, it's teacher Richard Vernon's turn to learn something from Carl. The frustrated Vernon, played by actor Paul Gleason, grumbles about how arrogant the kids have become over the years. Carl reminds Vernon that he is the one who has actually changed, not the kids:

Carl the janitor: "If you were sixteen, what would you think of you?"

Teacher Vernon: "Now this is the thought that wakes me up in the middle of the night, that when I get older, these kids are gonna take care of me."

Carl the janitor: "I wouldn't count on it."

As both Ted Marchbanks and Richard Vernon learned, treating people poorly because we think we're better than them can later come back to haunt us.

It takes a lot of energy and effort to be "on" all the time, but the great ones never turn it off. Marshall Goldsmith personally observed former President Bill Clinton many times and "it didn't matter if you were a head of state or a bell clerk, when you were talking with Bill Clinton he acted as if you were the only person in the room." Arguably the most powerful man in the world, President Clinton might shake hands or talk with hundreds of people in a day. And as exhausting as that may seem, for each of these brief encounters, "he conveyed how important you were, not how important *he* was." Clinton knew many of those people would remember meeting the president for the rest of their lives, and he made sure to leave a positive first impression on everyone. If he could accomplish that while leading the free world, certainly we could all give it a shot.

My two biggest influences in business have been my father and my father-in-law. Both had very different styles but were strikingly similar in how they treated people. They took the time to interact with everyone, whether it was within their own companies or visiting someone else's. My dad always engaged in brief, lively conversations with the drive-thru attendants at fast-food restaurants, and my kids crack up when I do the same today. What I learned watching these two men was to treat everyone equally. Unlike Ted Marchbanks, I am always aware that the person getting the coffee for this meeting may be the key decision maker at the next one. The guy in the shorts and flip-flops may be related to the owner—or, better yet, they may *be* the owner! You never know who is watching, or why it might be important to you.

Ralph Waldo Emerson said, "In my walks, every man I meet is my superior in some way, and in that I learn from him." Keep Carl the janitor fresh in your mind whenever you meet someone new. Every one of us has lived a life and has unique stories to tell. Instead of dismissing someone as a waste of our time, we should try to identify what it is they might be able to teach us. At the very least, we will have a left a positive first impression. After all, we never know who might be watching.

Under the Influence: Our Inner Circle

*Show me your friends
and I'll show you your future.*

—ANONYMOUS

Motivational speaker Jim Rohn famously said, "You are the average of the five people you spend the most time with." This should underscore once again just how important our relationships are. Take a moment to think about the five people you spend the most time around. What are their values? Are they successful? Are they supportive? Do they inspire you? We often assume we have good instincts about those we surround ourselves with, but how well do we really understand the magnitude of their impact on us?

Harvard's David McClelland is considered one of the most eminent psychologists of the 20th century following fifty years of research on human motivation and achievement. According to McClelland, the single most important factor in our success is the makeup of our "reference group." A reference group may be thought of as our inner circle, the people we spend the most time with. Looking at twenty-five years of data, McClelland discovered reference groups can determine up to 95 percent of success or failure in life. Our closest relationships influence us more than anything else, and we should expect to gravitate toward the levels of those individuals. This means when we spend time with those who don't seem to be seeking their full potential, we are pulled down. When we associate with those who strive for bigger things, we are lifted higher. Surrounding ourselves with encouragement and positive influences is essential for personal growth and happiness.

Successful and motivated individuals not only model ideal behaviors for us, but also allow us to learn their effective habits and principles. Most winners have gone through challenges and are willing to help us do the same. Soon after leading North Carolina to a college basketball championship, Michael Jordan was drafted by a lackluster Chicago Bulls team in 1985. He immediately began changing the culture of the entire organization. His commitment to hard work, discipline, and success forced every player on his teams to become better. After winning three championships as a player with Jordan in Chicago, Steve Kerr eventually won two more as head coach of the Golden State Warriors. One of those Warriors team even broke the single season wins record that Kerr helped set as a Bulls player. How important was Jordan's influence on him? "I owe him everything," Kerr said.

I recently experienced the incredible power of influence during a steps challenge at work. I joined several colleagues in competing to see who could walk the most over a two-month period. Seeing the updated steps leaderboard pushed me to walk more throughout each day, which in turn pushed others to walk more. In the end, one person won the actual prize, but we all ended up winners because everyone got in better shape. We motivated each other to make ourselves better. This is precisely the type of environment we cultivate in all areas of our lives by surrounding ourselves with the right people. It's far too easy to be complacent and lazy when our inner circle normalizes negative behavior.

Protecting our inner circle is critical, and there are three types of people we must work to keep out of it. We've all heard how one bad apple spoils the bunch, and nowhere is this truer than with our closest relationships.

The first type of person we should avoid is the one with an inherently negative disposition. Negativity is like a drug addiction; there may be a temporary comfort found in commiserating with another person, but we still feel crappy when it's over. Negative people don't want others to succeed because it makes them feel worse about themselves. Once our negative friends feel threatened by our success, they will turn on us, too. They are often needy, demanding, and make us feel guilty. The more time we spend with them, the more our own happiness and feelings of accomplishment will be drained.

Second is the narcissist, and I have had the misfortune of dealing with more than one. The term is often casually applied to someone egotistical or self-centered. The true narcissist is a far greater concern, which is why we must be alert for the following warning signs:

- They have a grandiose sense of self-importance.
- They live in a fantasy world.
- They need constant praise or admiration.
- They feel entitled to special treatment.
- They exploit others without guilt or shame.

Narcissists believe they are superior to everyone else and rules do not apply to them. They treat the people in their lives as tools to get what they want. They have no empathy toward others, and they will only pretend to care when it benefits them in some way. Narcissists feel threatened by people who have things they lack or who challenge them. They can become nasty and vindictive. They often find themselves in conflicts.

Narcissists worm their way into our lives through their incredible confidence and charm. They often appear generous and thoughtful in the beginning, but this is sheer manipulation. One way to identify a potential narcissist is by the absence of long-term close friendships. Because they are deficient in forming lasting relationships, they burn a person and move on to someone new. Or worse, they find an endlessly believing person who cannot get away. Once we've identified a narcissist, we need to establish some serious boundaries or extricate them completely from our lives. The longer we allow them to remain in our inner circles, the more damage they will do.

Trust me: You can't game plan against crazy. Avoid these people at all costs.

The third person to avoid are the timesuckers. Unlike negative people and narcissists, timesuckers don't always have bad intentions. In fact, they are often quite generous and thoughtful. The problem with timesuckers is they place greater expectations on us than we are willing or able to meet. Timesuckers want full recaps and explanations about our daily interactions. They want to get together far more often than we do. Timesuckers are challenging because we always want caring people in our lives, but these relationships tend to skew toward an unhealthy imbalance. There are only two ways we can sustain a relationship with a timesucker: We either set boundaries and hope to find an acceptable equilibrium, or we slowly manage them out of our inner circle.

All relationships evolve over time, and our inner circles will as well. People and circumstances never stay the same. Our components of time never stay the same. Think of the music bands that stay together for generations. They cannot write the same songs today they did earlier in their careers. They are different people with different perspectives now. Our interests and priorities are constantly developing, and we need to make sure the people around us are aligned with them. We accomplish this by prioritizing time spent around the kind of people we want to be, and minimizing time spent with those who are on a different path.

Changing the nature of an important relationship is never easy to do, and it can leave some powerful emotions in its wake. By treating a person with class and dignity, we can create space for ourselves without leaving hurt or anger behind us. Both personal and professional relationships ebb and flow, they may cool off and then strengthen again in the future. Not every breakup is final, and for that reason we should never burn the bridge that leads back to us. Emotion should never lead us to disparage someone with whom we've shared a part of our lives.

The initial sadness and rejection will fade over time, and the positive aspects will shine brightly. Leaving insults and anger in our wake will only justify those for feeling glad we are gone. Remember the value of the "positive close" from earlier. Our last actions are often the most memorable.

Lastly, we must remember why it is called an *inner circle*. We are in it together. Each of us serves as a key influencer for those close to us. Our values and our behaviors determine whether we belong or not. Just as we reap the benefits from the positive attributes of others, we must act in a manner deserving of the relationship if we expect to retain it.

Action Exercise

Identify your inner circle. Who are the five people you spend the most time with? Do they represent your values? Do they motivate you to be a better person? Is there anyone in this circle who might be contributing to holding you back? What changes might you make at this point about who you spend your time with?

17

Family

Family is not an important thing.
It's everything.

—MICHAEL J. FOX,
AMERICAN ACTOR

As children, we have no control over the family we are born into. Once we become adults, however, we have the opportunity to shape the type of family we want. We can decide whether or not to get married, whether or not to have children, and how many children we want to have. Most of all, we can determine the kind of relationships we will have with all these people. They are typically the most meaningful relationships in our lives.

Dating

The French philosopher Voltaire reportedly said, "the perfect is the enemy of the good." Holding out for the perfect mate is a recipe for lifelong disappointment. This may draw the ire of hopeless romantics, but the concept of just one soul mate for each person unfortunately is a myth. Consider the following tale from Middle Eastern folklore:

Mulla Nasrudin was talking with a friend about his love life. "I thought I had found the perfect woman," Mulla said. "She was beautiful and had the most pleasing features a man could imagine. She was exceptional in every way, except she had no knowledge."

"So I traveled farther and met a woman who was both beautiful and intelligent. But, alas, we couldn't communicate."

"After further travels, I met a lady who had everything: perfect mind, perfect intelligence, and great beauty, all the features I was looking for, but..."

"What happened?" asked the friend. "Why didn't you marry her at once?"

"Ah well," said Mulla, "as luck would have it, she was looking for the perfect man."

We often forget that the primary reason we have romantic relationships is to enrich our lives. Dating affords us the opportunity to get to know people and share experiences on a more intimate level. A healthy relationship allows us to continue growing as individuals while sharing our journey with another person. When our own priorities become stifled as a result of our companionship, it's only a matter of time before the relationship ends. Regardless of how long two people have been together, there is no obligation to stick it out when a relationship ceases to benefit both. Instead of avoiding the pain of a breakup, we should view it in its proper context. Remember that each relationship teaches us more about who we are and what we are looking for. Being willing to share so much, and risk the hurt of it not working out, ultimately gets us closer to finding the ideal intimacy and enrichment we seek with another partner.

You may be among the few who marry their high school sweetheart, but the odds are stacked against it. Young people are still figuring out who they are, all the while constantly evolving. On top of that, they have absolutely no idea what a mature relationship looks and feels like. Some lose their individual identities and throw all their self-worth into the "us" of a couple. Others are too focused on their own desires to reasonably make room for another person in their lives. Finding that ideal balance between codependency and selfishness takes experience and learning from painful mistakes. Falling in love is filled with euphoric emotions that can throw all of our priorities out of whack. We can become enthralled with these powerful feelings and, worst of all, we may not be able to imagine ever having those feelings about another person. That is why breaking up is so difficult. However, each time we become wrapped inside the thrill of love and then endure the pain of loss, we gain valuable insights about ourselves and what matters most to us in a relationship. We will carry that additional wisdom and perspective with us when we search for our next partner.

Regardless of how long they last, the majority of relationships will eventually run their course. Our personal growth should always be a priority, and we should never shortchange ourselves by staying with someone who rows against that current. Life changes over time and so do we. We need to recognize when it feels like the relationship is pulling us down more than lifting us up, and take the difficult steps to move on. Fear of being alone is a poor excuse to prolong an unhealthy relationship. Begging someone not to leave is pathetic. A relationship requires a healthy balance between two people with an equal desire to remain together. When those conditions no longer exist, both parties need to accept it. Major life changes are scary, but that is often precisely where our biggest leaps forward come from.

In *The Subtle Art of Not Giving a F*ck*, Mark Manson argues that the mark of a healthy relationship is how well each person accepts responsibility for themselves. We need to handle our own problems and not require the other person to solve them for us. This can only occur with healthy boundaries in place. Healthy boundaries enable direct and honest communication without fear of arguments, tantrums, and retribution. "If you make a sacrifice for someone you care about," Manson explains, "it needs to be because you want to, not because you feel obligated or because you fear the consequences of not doing so." Changing some of our behaviors to better fit into a relationship is a reasonable expectation, but changing our values is a bridge too far.

There are also unhealthy pairings in which two people appear to complement each other perfectly but, in reality, each person may be missing something important from the relationship. One example is the "victim" and the "solver." Victims get attention by creating problems for others to fix and solvers feel most valued when they can fix other people's problems. Such personalities are often drawn to each other. Even though each feels they have found the perfect counterpart, over time they will only perpetuate their own deficiencies. A relationship built on obligation and expectation denies both people the opportunity to experience true fulfillment, along with the growth and enjoyment they deserve.

Those in a healthy relationship are willing to be honest with each other about their problems without fearing the destruction of the relationship. We all have baggage and issues we work through, and they become even more evident when we spend more of our time with another person. Neither of us should expect the other person to do the work we need to do ourselves. If I am overly controlling, possessive, manipulative, distrusting, withdrawn, or some other unhealthy behavior, that is a *me* problem that I need to fix. If my partner has one of these issues and is unable or unwilling to work through it, then the obvious decision for me is to move on. Neither love nor fear of loss are good enough reasons to stay in an unhealthy situation. We owe it to each other to carry our own water and not be an impediment to our partner's growth.

The sad reality is that most romantic relationships will end, but they should never be viewed as a waste of our time. Marilyn Monroe said, "Never regret anything, because at one time it was exactly what you wanted." The legendary actress certainly knew the importance of exiting the stage gracefully, and so should we. It is often difficult and painful to accept the ending when it comes, but a horrible breakup will tarnish what was otherwise a meaningful relationship. Besides, I once learned that an ex-girlfriend of mine actually spoke positively about me to another girl. It made me wish I had handled the ending of other relationships with the same maturity and grace.

Marriage

> *Love is an ideal thing, marriage is a real thing.*
>
> —JOHANN WOLFGANG VON GOETHE,
> GERMAN AUTHOR AND PLAYWRIGHT

Instead of being viewed as the inevitable next step in a long-term relationship, marriage should only be considered when two people are able to develop a healthy, balanced partnership. Somewhere between 39 to 50 percent of marriages end in divorce, but that figure gets even more depressing when we consider how many unhappy marriages never actually end. This is precisely why it is so critical to figure out the dating part before signing ourselves up for life. Any lingering doubts whether you're with the right person, or whether you want to share your life forever, will only intensify over time. Marriage is often challenging, frustrating, stressful, and painful even under the best of circumstances. Though it requires constant effort and management, it should result in the most rewarding relationship with another person we will ever have.

Before considering marriage, it is critical to really understand each other's views about the future. Priorities change dramatically once two people are married. When I was dating, I primarily made decisions based upon what was in my own best interest. I wasn't ultimately responsible for how those decisions affected another person. For example, I didn't need my girlfriend's permission to accept a job in another city. Once I got married, however, big decisions were no longer mine to make alone. Moving cities would require my wife to find new work, leave her friends and family, and build new relationships. Every major decision once we are married directly impacts someone else we promised to share our life with. It adds another layer of complication and obligation.

Entering adulthood is exciting because much of it is unpredictable and the possibilities seem endless. We may begin our careers with specific plans and dreams, but often along the way, we experience major professional changes. Some people become wealthy while others wrestle with financial setbacks. Some people enjoy their work while others change careers entirely. There are very different definitions of success and the paths taken to find it. When a relationship gets serious, there must be a conversation to ensure the values, goals, and expectations of the future of both partners are aligned. If there is a serious disconnect at the beginning of the marriage, it will only lay the groundwork for disappointment and blame later on.

It may be uncomfortable and slightly scary to share our visions of the future with each other, but we'd better have a clear idea of what our spouses think they're getting out of the deal. There should be an honest exchange of views on major topics like living locations, lifestyle preferences, finances, employment, children, and religion. Are each person's expectations reasonable? Will there be enough money to pay for those expectations? What if there isn't? If two people aren't comfortable enough to have this discussion, they aren't ready to get married.

Being clear up front is so important because when a person later feels forced to make unexpected sacrifices or change their values to make a marriage work, there will be resentment toward their spouse. Because human beings are proven to be overly optimistic about our futures, we too often just assume, "Hey, it will all work out just fine." Failing to plan is planning to fail. It is far less painful to have this crucial conversation than to risk hearing your spouse later tell you, "This just isn't the life I expected to be living."

Once our expectations are aligned, and the knot has been tied, we must continually protect the two essential elements of every successful marriage: trust and respect. When one of them is missing, the marriage is in grave danger. Unfortunately, an inability to fully trust or respect a spouse may be a psychological holdover from childhood or a previous relationship. Remember: It is our responsibility to carry our own water in a relationship. We must address our own issues with self-reflection, a strong commitment to change, and perhaps even some difficult work in therapy if that's what it takes. Trust and respect are the highest priorities of a healthy marriage, and they are very difficult to repair once they've been damaged.

Trusting our spouse is having the willingness to be vulnerable with them. We must feel supported enough to share our deepest fears and insecurities. It can be a scary proposition for many people, but this raw openness is essential for maintaining that special bond. Trusting is believing we have each other's best interest at heart, and that honesty will always exist between us. Trusting allows each of us to continue growing as individuals, helping us learn from our mistakes without being punished for them.

A lack of trust manifests itself in suspicion, excessive anger, and controlling behavior. It poisons the relationship and undermines most of the benefits of sharing our lives with another person.

Along with trust, we must have mutual respect for each other. Respect maintains a shared balance of power in the marriage. It blossoms from appreciating our spouse for who they are and not being disappointed in who they are not. Respect is being proud of them and feeling grateful for them. It is genuinely listening with interest to what they have to say and not minimizing their intelligence or perspective. A marriage with mutual respect is full of surprises and favors done purely out of thoughtfulness. Respect means not taking the other person for granted.

Respect and resentment are a seesaw: as one goes down the other rises. Growing resentment, as noted earlier, is the great destroyer of relationships. Less respect leads to less communication. As a result, we stop caring enough to have the conversations required to resolve issues and remain supportive. We have troubling thoughts like, "It isn't worth having this conversation," "I don't feel like fighting about it," or "He/she wouldn't understand." We are denied crucial explanations and apologies, leaving hurt, frustration, and anger to smolder. We begin secretly blaming the other person for our unhappiness. The small crack that formed between us grows into a canyon and, as we are pulled apart, the threads of the relationship fray and unravel. Only by prioritizing mutual respect for each other can we maintain the special connection that enables our marriage to thrive.

Recall the earlier of tale Mulla Nasrudin, who failed in his search for the perfect woman, and consider this piece of advice about marriage: Never criticize your spouse for their shortcomings or their mistakes. Remember it is because of their faults and weaknesses they could not find a better spouse than you.

Sex: the thing that takes up the least amount of time and causes the most amount of trouble.

—John Barrymore,
American actor

Physical Intimacy

There is an elephant in the bedroom, and I've purposely saved it for last. The topic of physical intimacy may be uncomfortable to some, but it is an important component of marriage we all will eventually need to confront. Expectations about our physical relationships are a common source of frustration and tension in plenty of marriages. Remember when I said human beings are overly optimistic about their futures? The fact is, no matter how attracted we are to our spouse, no matter how in love we are, we simply aren't going to be nearly as physically intimate as we think we will. The good news is we aren't alone. In a recent study of 20,000 married couples, only 26 percent of them reported having sex once a week with the majority of them doing it less than twice a month.

Young couples with active libidos cannot envision a future scenario when they might actually have to motivate themselves to be romantic with each other, which is why they are so often unprepared for it when it happens. We blame our partners, our kids, or our work demands, but we rarely consider what could likely be the key to why marriages tend to become more platonic over time: our natural biology.

If we consider the possibility that men and women were not designed to settle down with just one person for the rest of their lives, we might begin to understand some of these frustrated feelings better. Humans consider themselves special, but we are extremely rare among all species for attempting monogamy. Christopher Ryan and Cacilda Jethá explored this topic in their book *Sex at Dawn*. Their research concluded, "No group-living nonhuman primate is monogamous, and adultery has been documented in every human culture studied, including those in which fornicators are routinely stoned to death. In light of all this bloody retribution, it's hard to see how monogamy comes 'naturally' to our species."

Robert Sapolsky noted his similar findings in *Behave*, "Most cultures have historically allowed polygamy—unions with more than one spouse, with monogamy as the rarer beast." These theories suggest that while the concept of marriage between two people has become normal in our society, it certainly isn't *natural* in our brains. Just as our stress responses remain programmed for survival in our ancestors' world, is it possible our bodies retain an encoded motivation to procreate with multiple partners? This could help explain one of the primary reasons why monogamy often leads to monotony. Marriage may set up an inevitable conflict between society and biology, without a perfect solution to satisfy both.

This theory suggests our genes don't care nearly as much about love and commitment as they do about replicating themselves. Being programmed to crave sexual variety for that reason would explain why we find ourselves admiring attractive strangers. Our traditional marriages, therefore, deny us the actual fulfillment of these basic physiological needs. Ryan and Jethá conclude that "marriage is a failure. Emotionally, economically, psychologically, and sexually, it just doesn't work over the long term for too many couples." They are supported by a recent poll revealing that the top two reasons cited for divorce were lack of commitment and infidelity.

The solution advocated by *Sex at Dawn* is a flexible, open marriage where we can keep our life partners without denying ourselves our natural physical desires. Perhaps that concept works for some spouses, without leaving emotional devastation in its wake, but for many of us (including me) it doesn't.

The fact is that human beings wrestle with genetic programming and natural urges all the time. Our bodies and brains were built for a much different way of life than we have today. Long before wedding vows and honeymoons, humans traveled around in groups and didn't own any property. We didn't maintain busy schedules and we didn't have stacks of bills coming due. During the Stone Age, sex was not exclusive to two people; it was frequently used by men *and* women for social purposes including stress reduction, conflict resolution, protection, and entertainment. Fast-forward through the agricultural, industrial, and technological revolutions, and we find ourselves today in a very different world. If our internal equipment still struggles to adapt to changing norms and environments, it's no wonder we get so frustrated.

Although there may actually be a plausible biological excuse for marital transgressions, it is highly unlikely to soften the feelings of betrayal they will cause. Mutual trust and respect are the two vital organs in a healthy marriage, and an affair demolishes both at once. The day may come when our brains actually evolve to reject our adulterous tendencies but until then we would be wise to accept reality and work within its confines. We can acknowledge that our libidos may occasionally be disconnected from our love for our partners. There are crossed wires inside each of us, but better communication and understanding are the keys to seeing it through together.

This potentially controversial detour leads us back to our original conclusion: We must give serious thought to our individual priorities and expectations before entering into marriage. If the intensity of physical intimacy is one of the primary allures of the relationship, consider what a future with that diminished might feel like for you. In addition, very few of us retain the same measure of youthful fitness and attractiveness over time. Unfortunately, I am only aware of two ways to continue dating a young and attractive person: avoiding marriage or multiple divorces. If neither of those options is appealing, be realistic about what lies ahead of you.

Marriage may be imperfect and often challenging, but it is truly a rare gift to be treasured. It tests us, shapes us, and provides opportunities for incredible joy. The decision to marry should be made with an eye to the future, based on partnership and mutual support. When our best friend is by our side, it makes the good times better and the bad times more tolerable. There is nothing more meaningful than waking up each day next to the person who has chosen to spend the rest of their life with us. It is without question the most valuable relationship we can have.

Children

Children are not a distraction
from more important work.
They are the most important work.

—Dr. John Trainer,
FAMILY PHYSICIAN

There are no relationships in life like the ones we have with our children. Think about it: We meet a person on the day they are born, when they are completely dependent on us for everything. We spend several years teaching, disciplining, supporting, guiding, chaperoning, worrying, loving, and enjoying them—all while slowly preparing them to eventually leave us.

There is a relatively small window when all parents have complete control over their kids' schedules. Unfortunately, children often enter the picture during the busiest times of our lives, and we share a lot of that window with our many other responsibilities. As young parents, we are often still figuring out who we are ourselves at the same time we begin shaping the life of another person. While building our careers, fretting over finances, and attempting to cling to remnants of the social lives we used to have, we often take for granted just how quickly our babies become young adults.

From the day they are born, the clock begins ticking. First birthday, first words, first steps, preschool, elementary school, carpools, practices, games, lessons, recitals, middle school, puberty, high school, driver's license, graduation, then *boom...*it's over. They are no longer fully under our control. Before long, they have a career and family of their own. The little kid who used to climb into our bed during a thunderstorm and call us for rides home doesn't need us anymore. Whatever kind of relationship we will have when they are adults is up to them, and that is going to depend heavily on the kind of legacy we left as a parent.

All parents with young children should be required to listen to the song "Cat's in the Cradle" by Harry Chapin. It is a father's portrayal of his relationship with his son over the years, and how his early choices come back to haunt him. It begins with the young boy idolizing his father and vowing, "I'm gonna be like you, Dad." The boy continually asks to do things with his father, who makes promises but never makes the time. Yet, despite being constantly neglected throughout his childhood, the boy still wants to be just like his father.

When the young man returns home from college, and the father now asks to spend a little time with him, the son has already made plans to be with his friends. Finally, the stinging rebuke comes at the end of the song with the father retired and the son living in another city with his own family. The old man calls to inquire about getting together. Caught up in his own life now, the son says he'd love to, but he's too busy and just doesn't have the time. At that moment, the father painfully realizes his son made good on his promise: "He'd grown up just like me." It is a sad, but indispensable, reminder that our kids learn how to set their priorities by our example.

Raising kids is the Olympic Games of priority setting. They begin life completely reliant on us for everything, as little-by-little we prepare them to one day replace us in the world. We shape them every day by the environment we maintain, the type of discipline we instill, and the evolving relationships we carve out with them. Children are our living legacies, and we all wish for them to find success and happiness in their own lives. Unfortunately, we often overlook the significance of our roles in that process. What types of behavior do we think we are modeling versus what they are actually interpreting? Whom do they trust for guidance and support? Where do they spend their time and learn their lessons? How valued do they feel as individuals? Are we helping them discover their own paths in life or steering them toward ones we've chosen for them?

There are different schools of thought on raising children and I will not attempt to lay out any specific set of instructions. There is no one-size-fits-all set of rules that works for every parent and every kid. However, of all the different parenting styles, the ones that work include the same two key elements. In order to have a healthy relationship with our kids, we must *care* and *be there.*

Does it sound simple? Of course. Do we find ways to royally mess it up? Absolutely. Raising children requires significant commitments of time, energy, and discipline. If we truly want to care and be there for our kids, we must make them a high priority.

To *care* is to make our children feel welcomed and appreciated. It means being supportive and invested in their development. It's remembering they're young and answering their endless questions without annoyance. It's showing them that their happiness is important to us. To care is also to prepare them for life. It's being willing to

149

upset them by setting and enforcing rules. It's expanding our level of trust when they've earned it. It's allowing them to make mistakes and helping them learn from them. To care is to be willing to make unexpected sacrifices of our own when they need us.

To *be there* is to show our child we're interested in what they do, even if we don't always understand it. It's putting the phone down, being an audience, teaching them something, playing a game. It's working with them to develop skills and pursue interests. It's being the face in the stands and the voice that says, "I enjoyed watching you perform." It's knowing when to let go of their hand and when to help them back up. Just being there is not the same thing as *being there*. Kids need our presence mentally, not just physically. Once that childhood window of time closes, it's too late. Just ask my mom.

My parents began dating in high school and apparently didn't figure out they should not have stayed together until after they had three kids. When I was growing up, there was a lot of arguing and yelling in our house. My dad moved out when I was seven, but the arguing and yelling continued without him. My mom has always had a huge heart, but back then she had a difficult time managing her anger, frustrations, and insecurities. I know my dad loved my mom until the day he died but, unfortunately, they just weren't compatible. He always tried his best to take care of her, even after he remarried, but my mom was frequently upset and stressed out. I do have many fun memories, but it was not always the happiest home to grow up in.

It was only when I had a family of my own that I began to see my childhood through my mom's eyes. What I can appreciate now, but didn't understand then, was that her entire life had been upended. Her relationship with my dad had been rocky, but it had always endured. She never expected the shock of it actually ending. In addition to rebuilding her personal life, she had to focus on a career, make dinners everyone complained about, clean up a messy house, and attend to the needs of three young kids by herself. This certainly wasn't the life she dreamed about, and I know it became even more frustrating for her when my dad got remarried.

With the benefit of maturity, experience, and self-reflection, I am now able to view my childhood in a much different context than I saw it years ago. I realize I unfairly favored my dad, who spoiled us, took us to do fun things, and then dropped us off at home. I recognize my mom is no longer the same person she was when I was little. She is a kind and gentle woman, often tearing up with pride just looking at her children and grandchildren. She also tears up with regret when we talk about the past, and those are the moments that hurt the most. I know she wishes she could do it over, and I really wish she could, too. Childhood trauma can have painful and long-lasting consequences on a person's self-confidence and future relationships.

Even with the proper clarity and understanding, it's not always easy for me to put the pieces neatly back together. I now live in another city with my own family and, though I love my mom very much, I do a terrible job of staying in touch with her. I often think of *Cat's in the Cradle,* and how similar my life is to the adult son's life in the song. It is incredibly difficult to overcome the deep imprints left from these early experiences, even when we really want to.

As they develop, kids tend to mimic many of the behaviors modeled by their parents. In my case, I learned to release my anger by yelling. I have worked very hard to change this behavior and channel my frustrations without hurting someone else's feelings. Thanks to a patient wife and three very insightful kids, I am better able to recognize my anger sooner and dial it down. I'm certainly not perfect, but I will never give up trying to do better. Children need self-confidence to navigate their adolescence, and we forget how easy it can be for parents to break it. Remember: Making children a priority isn't just showing up and going through the motions. We have to remember that the things we do, and the way we do them, have an enormous long-lasting impact.

Young boys should never be sent to bed. They always wake up a day older, and then before you know it, they've grown.

—J.M. BARRIE,
SCOTTISH CREATOR OF PETER PAN

How many times have you raced through children's books just to get through the story and send the kids to bed? How often have you said, "It's time to go inside now," before it was really time? Just so we can get on to something else, we hurry our children through these moments without realizing how meaningful they actually are. Finding the right balance between kid time and grown-up time is challenging, but every day our window is closing. Slowly at first, and then it comes crashing shut. As our children get older, they will choose to spend more and more time with their friends, leaving less and less time for us. While that may occasionally seem like it will be a welcome relief, we may find ourselves longing for the time they still viewed us as their main source of companionship and entertainment. And then it's too late to go back.

Remember: *Care* and *be there*. Special experiences don't have to cost a lot. Some of my fondest memories include family movie nights, dance parties, domino rallies, puzzles, board games, sledding, fishing, backyard sports, and living room forts. I wouldn't trade any of those experiences for a trip to the Super Bowl, unless my kids would be there with me. Stacey and I will be empty nesters one day, and we will have the rest of our lives to pursue our own interests. Our kids are our highest priorities now.

One final note about balance: *Not being there enough* for our kids is one mistake but *being there too much* is another. There comes a time when we have to loosen up and allow them to grow up. After devoting so much of ourselves to raising our children, it is often difficult for some of us to no longer be needed. We forget that our responsibility as parents is to raise adults, not children. Adults are capable of managing their own relationships and making decisions about their lives without our controlling them. Guilting our kids about not spending enough time with us, or how unimportant they make us feel, will not motivate them to want us around. On this I speak from personal experience. It is far better to be periodically desired than constantly avoided. The parameters will shift over time, but we can always find new ways to care and be there for our children.

Action Exercise

Let your kids plan a family night. Pick a free night and devote it entirely to your kids. Let them have input on dinner and let them pick a fun activity or two. Keep the phones, work, and grown-up stuff out of the way until bedtime. And let bedtime come when the fun is over, not when the clock tells you. When they ask to do it again, you'll know it was successful.

Relationships: Summary

Our relationships are second only to time in the things that matter most. How we choose and allocate our time among our relationships will define our life's experiences, our successes, and our happiness.

- Every relationship we choose to have throughout our lives is a product of how closely we understand ourselves.

- Our perspective is the lens we look through to see the world around us. We should focus only on the things we can control, and we should ignore the things we cannot.

- Anger is a natural human emotion we can learn to manage by recognizing when it is no longer helping us.
- Resentment is a slow-burning bitterness we allow to build up over time when we fail to resolve our issues. It is the great destroyer of relationships.
- When we worry about things that might not happen and that are outside our control, we punish ourselves unnecessarily.
- Not only are we unreliable forecasters about future outcomes, but we are also terrible at estimating today how we might feel about them later.
- The ability to demonstrate confidence, even when nervous or afraid, will have the most impact on a person's success and relationships.
- Learning to overcome the fear of rejection opens many doors and boosts actual confidence.
- We don't know what we don't know. Only by accepting the possibility of being wrong and being open to new information will we learn and develop wisdom.
- There are differences between acquaintances and friends. Both serve important roles, but we must be mindful of how we allocate our time among them.
- Relationships are born when we are willing to meet new people. We hurt ourselves by not taking advantage of these opportunities.
- First impressions happen quickly but last a long time. Remember CLIP to do it right:
    - project *confidence*

- *listen*
- be *interested*
- *positive* close

- Building relationships the right way requires:
  - thoughtfulness
  - generosity
  - genuineness

- You never know who is watching. We must treat everyone with kindness and respect, regardless of whether we think they can help us or not.

- Our inner circle is responsible for the majority of our successes and failures in life. Do the five people we spend the most time with represent who we want to be? Do they share our values and motivate us?

- Our own personal growth should never be sacrificed in a healthy relationship. A proper balance is maintained only when both people can grow together as individuals.

- Before getting married, both people should have an honest conversation about their values, expectations, and vision for the future.

- There may be biological forces working against our ability to maintain a high level of physical intimacy with the same person over a long period of time. We need to prepare for the physical relationship we have with our spouse to inevitably wane. This will require understanding and communication.

- Trust and respect are the two vital elements of every successful marriage.

- Children often internalize the behavior of their parents. How we prioritize our kids will influence the kind of relationship we have with them later on.

- Our children grow up in the blink of an eye. Our future relationships with them depends a lot on the kind of relationship we have with them when they are younger.

- Whatever parenting style we choose to implement, the two key elements are to *care* and *be there*.

- Inevitably, our children won't need us anymore, and it is our job to prepare them for it. We have a window of time when we have them all to ourselves, and beyond that we should avoid guilting them for becoming independent.

Part III

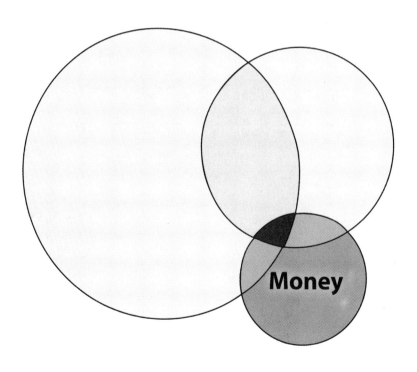

18

We've Been Misled

*Nowadays people know the price of everything
and the value of nothing.*

—OSCAR WILDE,
IRISH POET AND PLAYWRIGHT

The third thing that matters most to us is money, but not in the way most of us are used to thinking about it. Our culture leads us to believe the wealthy live better than everyone else, but the reality is far different. Simply put, if we do not prioritize our time and our relationships first, all the money in the world will not buy our happiness. The man in the following story certainly wished he'd learned this sooner.

There was once a man whose goal was to be the richest person in the world. He worked every day and did not return home until after his children had gone to bed. As his wealth grew, he expanded his business and he rarely spent time with his family. He worked so hard that after several years, he did become one of the richest people in the world.

Then one day, the rich man was planning his retirement when he was visited by an angel of death. He had worked his entire life to acquire so much wealth he could retire in luxury, and he could not believe his time was up. Being one of the richest men in the world, he decided he would buy one more year from the angel of death no matter the cost. He continued bargaining for a while, but the angel was unmoved.

Desperate, the rich man made another proposal to the angel. He said, "Give me just one hour so I can admire the beauty of this world for the last time and spend some quality time with my family and friends, whom I have not seen in so long. For this I will leave you all my wealth." But the angel again refused.

Finally, the man begged the angel for one minute to write a good-bye note to his family. This wish was granted. The man's note read, "Spend the time you have in the right way. Listen to your heart, make sure the things around you have meaning and cherish every minute. Because once your time is up and death comes, you can't buy even an hour of life with all the money in the world."

If money could actually buy happiness, there wouldn't be so many miserable millionaires in the world. Blake Mycoskie was one of them. He sold half of his company, TOMS Shoes, for more than $300 million in 2014. Just in his 30s, Mycoskie had the ability to buy and do anything he wanted for the rest of his life. About a year later, he was diagnosed with mild depression. Mycoskie is hardly alone.

The wealthy cannot buy themselves a better life because it is the value of our personal connections that bring us happiness, not the value of our bank accounts. In *Tribe,* author Sebastian Junger underscores how we expect to be spiritually uplifted by the advantages and opportunities of living in a wealthy nation, but "as affluence and urbanization rise in a society, rates of depression and suicide tend to go *up* rather than down." The reasoning for this is actually quite simple: The more financially successful we become, the more we tend to isolate ourselves from others. Recall the boy from the story a previous chapter, who left his rich father's secluded mansion to visit the joyful people in the countryside. The less connected we are to others, the more our happiness and mental state suffers. No amount of money can buy our way out of that.

Money matters most when it covers our basic needs, protects us in times of emergency, and enables us to take advantage of life experiences. Money matters least when treated as a measurement of one's accomplishments or worth. Wealthy people are quick to credit their own skill and hard work for their financial advantages. They are often quite reluctant to admit the outsized role good luck has played in their own success, and even more reluctant to acknowledge how bad luck has influenced the lives of those less fortunate. An exception was J. Paul Getty, once the richest man in the world, who famously shared his formula for success: "Rise early, work hard, strike oil." It was the equivalent of saying, "Do your best and get really lucky."

No matter how well we play the game of life, some of us just get luckier than others. We have no control over the country we are born in or the wealth of our parents, but these two factors alone can mean the difference between a person becoming a neurosurgeon or a hospital custodian. Both the doctor and the janitor provide valuable services, but one makes significantly more money. Medical school is very expensive and requires years of studying. Having parents with means and a focus on education is a fortunate advantage not everyone is blessed with.

And yet, even without such advantages, so many people have started with nothing and created vast fortunes. Many others began with fortunes and found themselves with nothing. And some, like the legendary stock trader Jesse Livermore, have made and lost fortunes multiple times. We cannot account for luck, either our own or someone else's, so measuring our wealth against another's is a fool's errand. Only one scorecard truly matters: the decisions we've made for our own particular situation.

Life often plays out like the board game Chutes and Ladders, which demonstrates the impact of luck on our journeys. In the game, players roll the dice and move their pieces along in an attempt to reach the top of the board first. Along the way, the players randomly land on ladders that boost them ahead and chutes that drop them back. Some players land on a few big ladders early on and race out to a big lead while others slowly plod along. Just when a player appears to have an insurmountable lead, a big chute sends them sliding down below the others. In life, we also experience periods of progress and setbacks. Whether a hardship is minor or monumental, the majority of financial falters we may experience in life can be overcome with the right mind-set. We must understand we cannot grow personally or professionally without being willing to risk failure and work our way through it.

Hotelier Ian Schrager is a perfect example. He first hit it big with the legendary New York club Studio 54 in the late 1970s, and then went to prison for tax evasion. When he emerged, he was nearly $2 million in debt, with a criminal record. This level of failure would be extreme by any measure. However, he did not despair over all he had lost, and did not surrender hopes for a successful future. Schrager slowly rebuilt his career by putting one foot in front of the other. He didn't focus on how far he had to go or what could possibly go wrong. He certainly didn't allow the financial success of others to discourage him. He estimated it took nearly ten years just to get back to where he once was. Yet, eventually, he launched the boutique hotel revolution and found greater financial success than ever before. Ian Schrager paid an expensive price in time, but his story proves even large sums of money can eventually be replaced.

I have studied money, both personally and professionally, and gained many insights along the way. Above all else, I have concluded there is a universal guiding principle: Our views on money must fit within the framework we have first built around our time and relationships. Take another look at our Venn diagram and note the sizes of the three circles. The way we think about money may very well be ruining our lives now and setting us up for a painful future. Likewise, we need to shift our views on failure, which can be one of the best teachers we'll ever have. Constant preparation is key to our success, but part of the process is incorporating the lessons from our disappointments. We begin by answering the most important financial question of all.

19

Can Money Buy Happiness?

*How many people do you know who are spending
money they have not yet earned for things they don't
need, to impress people they don't like?*

—EDGAR ALLAN MOSS,
AMERICAN AUTHOR

The answer to whether or not money can buy happiness is this: It depends. As Yuval Harari concludes in *Sapiens,* "Money does indeed bring happiness. But only up to a point, and beyond that point it has little significance." If I am making $25,000 and struggling to pay my bills, doubling my income will substantially improve my living situation and have a long-lasting effect on my well-being. In this case, we have a strong argument that more money is directly tied to more happiness.

However, if I'm already making $175,000 a year and I get that same $25,000 raise, the short-term burst of excitement I will receive is likely to fade. Sure, I would be able to upgrade to more fancy things, but before long I will return to my previous level of happiness. Money provides diminishing returns much sooner than we realize. As a result, people who wrongly over-prioritize making more money are never able to fill the holes inside themselves with it. If we can't find true happiness and meaning in our lives once our basic needs are fulfilled, no amount of dollars will bring them to us.

Correlating our self-worth with the ability or the willingness to spend money is a recipe for disaster. Our culture of consumption continues fooling new generations into believing that the more we buy, the happier we will be. Magazines, reality television, and social media have opened a Pandora's box of anxiety, unleashing before our eyes a never-ending parade of lives well-lived. These cleverly edited sucker punches depress the value of our own existence by comparison. All the while, it turns out we just aren't comparing the right things.

Real happiness doesn't come from having what we want; it comes from wanting what we have. Studies continue to prove that our happiness actually depends far less on our objection condition of wealth than on its correlation with our subjective expectations. In other words, most of us really aren't unhappy because we don't *have* more money. We are unhappy because we *think* we should have more money. Even when we have plenty to be grateful for, seeing others with more makes us feel less important. It just doesn't seem fair that they can do and buy more than we can. This connects with our earlier discussion about envy and the importance of adjusting our perspective. When we use other people's money as the yardstick for measuring our own happiness, no amount will ever be enough to provide lasting and meaningful contentment.

The satirist H. L. Mencken said, "Wealth is any income that is at least one hundred dollars more than the income of one's wife's sister's husband." While humorous, this anecdote carries with it a healthy dose of caution. Research reveals that people would actually prefer earning a lower salary provided it is higher than that of their friends, rather than a higher salary which is lower than that of their friends. What kind of perspective leads us to willingly accept less money because it makes us feel better by comparison? If more money was truly the key to happiness, we couldn't possibly think this way.

To illustrate just how crazy this thinking is, if I were the person from the earlier example making $175,000 and getting the $25,000 raise, I would earn more than 90 percent of the rest of America. That is more money than three average American households combined. Nearly everywhere I go, I would be wealthier than most of the people around me. By all accounts, I should have felt happy and successful before the raise, but afterward I should feel it even more. However, if someone close to me—say my wife's sister's husband—were to receive a raise from $165,000 to $300,000, suddenly it's not such a big win for me anymore. My own situation just got better, but I'm more preoccupied with my inability to keep pace with the other guy. This type of thinking is the psychological poison we must train our minds to neutralize.

Once again: The only person we should compare ourselves to is the one staring back at us in the mirror. If we allow our happiness to be affected by what other people can buy, we will have forfeited control over our lives. We will always find people with more or less money than we have, and we can always choose how we want to feel about it. Three things matter most, and they all work together. Money may be the least important of the three, but it can have a ripple effect from the bottom up. By maintaining a healthier perspective about money, we will enrich our relationships and make much better use of our time. The opposite is also true. If we do not view money in its proper context, we will damage our relationships and waste the opportunities to enjoy our precious time here.

A turning point in my life was marked by a significant realization: True happiness is found by spending money on moments, not on material possessions. Like so many others, I used to prefer buying physical things because

I felt I'd get more value from them over a long period of time.

Fill your life with experiences, not things.
Have stories to tell, not stuff to show.

—ANONYMOUS

Experiences, on the other hand, happen and then are immediately gone, with nothing tangible left behind. In reality, the excitement, and often the utility, of new things fades quickly. We rarely have meaningful enough interactions with our possessions we can share interesting stories about. However, we can go on and on about the summer we rented an RV and drove across the country.

"Experiences make people happier than do possessions," journalist James Hamblin wrote in *The Atlantic*, "Even a bad experience becomes a good story." The key is learning to prioritize our moments and the memories they provide us.

Our experiences provide more happiness than our things because they are truly unique to each of us. As a result, we are less likely to measure our experiences against those of others. When the unhealthy tendency to compare is removed, we are rewarded with a pure enjoyment of what is ours. This is the difference between money and moments.

Further proof of this divergence can be found in the workplace. Whereas we would foolishly prefer earning a lower salary, provided it would still be higher than that of our peers, we see a far healthier dynamic play out when it comes to vacation days. Which of the following would you rather have?

- *Option 1:* You get two weeks of vacation and your peers get only one.

- *Option 2:* You get four weeks of vacation and your peers get six.

Studies have shown we would gladly prefer the four weeks, and we don't mind when our friends get six. Unlike dollars, we do not directly compare our vacation experiences with our friends, and we appreciate more time away regardless of what others receive. When we bypass the tangled wires in our brains, we recognize things do not deliver the level of happiness we get from experiences. The sooner in life we realize this, the better. "Many older people say they were so wrapped up in looking for what they didn't have that they seldom appreciated what they did have," Marshall Goldsmith tells us. "They often wish they would have taken more time to enjoy it."

These are certainly not new insights. People have allowed money to ruin their life's experiences since it was first put into circulation. "Prophets, poets, and philosophers realized thousands of years ago that being satisfied with what you already have is far more important than getting more of what you want," Harari reminds us in *Sapiens.* Not only do we reduce our overall happiness by focusing on what to buy next, but we can dig ourselves into holes we never even considered.

Very few of us accurately estimate the true cost of a major purchase, and end up wandering down a path of additional outlays we hadn't anticipated. For example, stretching to buy a lavish house might appear to work financially at the time of closing, but what about all the increased fixed costs we just locked ourselves into for years to come? Property taxes, insurance, utilities, landscaping, lawn care, and snow removal are all likely to cost more for a bigger house. More space also requires more furniture, more window treatments, more decorations, on and on. The creeping expenses from this one decision will not only reduce our ability to spend money on experiences, but they will also greatly impact our ability to save and invest our money for the future.

By overextending ourselves financially, we set ourselves on a tightrope over a heartbreaking valley below. No longer secure in our footing, one unexpected gust can send us tumbling to our shame. We can live happily without many things, but once we own them, we are devastated when we are forced to give them up. "Everywhere around us we see the temptation to improve the quality of our lives by buying a larger home, a second car, a new dishwasher, a lawn mower, and so on," Dan Ariely explains in *Predictably Irrational.* "But once we change our possessions, we have a very hard time going back down. Downgrading is experienced as a loss, and it is psychologically painful."

Living beyond our means is a highly effective method for jeopardizing our own happiness. Whenever we borrow money to buy things, we give up more control over our future. In *Stumbling on Happiness,* Daniel Gilbert warns, "Research has shown that when people lose their ability to control things, they become unhappy, helpless, hopeless, and depressed." Economies expand and contract, markets boom and bust, and events nobody saw coming can turn the world upside down. These events are called *black swans,* and they can be devastating. We may not see them coming, but we can reduce their impact on our lives by not being so imprudent with our money.

20

Black Swans and Bubbles

The problem with experts is that they do not know what they do not know.

—NASSIM NICHOLAS TALEB,
LEBANESE-AMERICAN ESSAYIST
AND RISK ANALYST

Because even experts don't know what they don't know, we are all prone to dismiss highly unlikely events as impossibilities. Or worse, we never even bother to consider them at all. These events are the black swans. "Black swans" derive their name from a time long ago, when all the swans in the world were believed to be white. Then, the sighting of a single black swan in Australia immediately shattered what had been a universally accepted fact for centuries. Black swan events lay bare the fallacy of drawing definitive conclusions based solely upon what has been observed to date.

Absence of proof is not proof of absence. Christopher Columbus had a similar blind spot in his thinking when he refused to consider the possibility of an undiscovered continent. It becomes far more dangerous for us when our trusted experts fail to account for black swans. We don't know what we don't know. Just because something has never happened before does not mean it cannot happen.

Obsessed with the concept of uncertainty since his childhood, Nassim Nicholas Taleb wrote a five-volume series about it called *The Incerto.* The second book, *The Black Swan,* focuses on these extremely powerful events that seemingly come out of nowhere. Taleb's black swan events have three defining characteristics: They are outliers that were not considered possible before they occurred, they carried an extreme impact, and people concocted explanations after the fact to make them seem predictable in retrospect. The 9/11 terrorist attack had all the elements of a black swan event. Nobody imagined that multiple planes could be hijacked and used as weapons. Thousands were killed, travel was forever changed, and a multiyear war in the Middle East began. Later, we learned of the supposed obviously missed clues, such as warnings received by the FBI about foreign men taking flight lessons with no interest in learning how to land the planes.

The 2007 financial crisis was another black swan. Risky home mortgages, which were then packaged and sold as investments, precipitated a systemic global melt-down, nearly sinking our entire financial system. Nobody expected a scenario in which legendary banks like Bear Stearns and Lehman Brothers would fail. Who could have imagined the worst recession since the Great Depression requiring an unprecedented government bailout?

Again, it all seemed so predictable after the fact. Home prices only seemed to go up. People were encouraged to enter into loans they didn't understand for houses they couldn't afford because banks had figured out how to make piles of money trading those loans. Once mortgage interest rates began climbing and home values began declining, the party was over. People could no longer refinance their mortgages or pull equity out of their houses to stay afloat. They began defaulting at alarming rates, banks suffered enormous losses, and the world economy imploded. Even with a long history of market bubbles to learn from, where were the experts to warn us something like this could happen?

The four most expensive words in the English language are, "This time is different."

—SIR JOHN TEMPLETON
AMERICAN-BRITISH INVESTOR

Mark Twain said, "History doesn't repeat itself, but it often rhymes." In the seventeenth century, a frenzy over tulip bulbs in the Netherlands caused many speculators to chase prices for these flowers higher and higher. One person reportedly offered twelve acres of land for a single bulb! When the tulip bubble eventually burst in 1637, prices plummeted, and many people were left financially ruined. Tulip Mania, the story of how people surrendered rationality and treated flowers as precious investments, was chronicled in Charles Mackay's 1841 classic *Extraordinary Popular Delusions and the Madness of Crowds*. If you don't read it, here is the key takeaway: When we blindly follow any crowd, it may lead us right off a cliff. It was true for the Dutch in the 1600s and it remains true today.

In 1995, little stuffed animals filled with plastic pellets called Beanie Babies gained popularity in Chicago, where I lived at the time. Thanks to the emergence of the Internet, a global market for Beanie Babies exploded on the popular auction Website eBay. Ty Warner, the creator of these plush pals, brilliantly released them in limited quantities and then retired them forever. This strategy caused certain coveted characters to change hands for thousands of dollars. Comparisons to the Tulip Mania were of course eventually made, but not before the bubble burst, and not before families lost fortunes "investing" in beanbags. In his documentary *Bankrupt by*

Beanies, Chris Robinson reveals the tragedy of his father sinking $100,000 into the plush pets, planning to fund his children's college tuitions with the extraordinary profits he expected to make. Bubbles seem ridiculous when viewed from a high level, but inside them it's another story. In fact, many people are well aware of what is happening. It is the uninformed who often suffer the most. As behavioral finance expert Morgan Housel explains in *The Psychology of Money,* "The formation of bubbles isn't so much about people irrationally participating in long-term investing. They're about people somewhat rationally moving toward short-term trading to capture momentum that had been feeding on itself." Someone buying and flipping for a quick profit has a very different mind-set than someone else buying for long-term value.

The damage from a bubble happens when long-term investors start taking cues from short-term momentum traders, who are playing a completely different game. Large sums of money were made by short-term tulip and Beanie Baby traders, but long-term investors were ruined. We cannot copy the financial activities of others when we don't fully understand the game they are playing. Remember this the next time you feel like joining the herd.

Black swans catch us off guard because we don't see them coming. Bubbles form when we ignore what we've already seen. One is "This can't happen" and the other is "This time is different." Both are extremely dangerous mind-sets that lead to irresponsible risk-taking and crushing financial blows. When experts have repeatedly failed to protect us from black swans and bubbles (and many led us right into them), we should be even more skeptical of being influenced by the behavior of our peers. We must be able to think for ourselves.

During the time I wrote this book, the world experienced another black swan. A deadly and highly contagious coronavirus called *COVID-19* rapidly spread throughout the world. The COVID-19 pandemic met all three requirements of a black swan event. It was certainly unexpected, at least here in the United States, where then-President Trump repeatedly suggested that nobody could ever have seen it coming. The extreme impact of the virus was obvious, with hundreds of thousands dead and an economy all but shut down. People avoided being in public and even feared visiting their loved ones. Lastly, even as the infection curve climbed higher, we began hearing the arguments that we should have seen it coming, and we should have been better prepared.

"Black Swan logic makes what you don't know far more relevant than what you do know," Taleb writes. We had no idea just how unprepared our governments and health-care infrastructures were to handle a pandemic of that magnitude. Never before had we experienced the canceling of entire sports seasons, the closings of schools across the country, or stores running out of toilet paper.

Who could have imagined a world in which people were genuinely afraid to leave their houses? Seemingly overnight, a booming economy and a record stock market were sent tumbling. Unemployment soared higher as many lost their jobs and their businesses. Even as the virus took hold in the United States, many of our own leaders downplayed the potential dangers to our health. How many of us were adequately prepared for the unimaginable?

The ugly stain on the world's richest economy is how many hardworking people live from paycheck to paycheck and struggle to keep their heads above water. Not only do the majority of our citizens save very little or nothing at all, but many are also living in perpetual debt. For these people, the pandemic turned their pursuit of the American Dream into an inconceivable nightmare.

Sadly, there was not much more a lot of these people could have done to protect themselves from this black swan. The same cannot be said for those of us who choose to live beyond our means, defenseless during times of uncertainty and upheaval. The people who prepare for a rainy day are the least likely to be washed away by a thousand-year flood.

Warren Buffett, legendary investor and one of the world's richest men, famously said, "Only when the tide goes out do you discover who's been swimming naked." An economy firing on all cylinders can mask a lot of poor decisions for a period of time. But those who are dangerously leveraged, or woefully unprepared, will meet their day of reckoning eventually. For clients of the fraudster Bernie Madoff, that day came during the 2008 financial crisis. Madoff had been able to maintain a $65 billion Ponzi scheme for two decades before the black swan market collapse brought his house of cards tumbling down. Movie stars, foundations, and many other innocent people lost everything they had. Certainly Madoff wasn't prepared for the expected chain of events unfolding to expose his scam so quickly and violently.

Far more importantly, his investors took startling risks by committing their entire life's savings to a con man, and blindly accepting his consistent reports of astonishing performance. Madoff's gift was his ability to create such a high degree of trust with his clients that many had even begged him to take their money! When people heard how much money their friends were supposedly making, the herd mentality kicked in, and they followed the crowd to their doom. The peculiarities of the fraudulent enterprise seemed obvious in the aftermath, but again, nobody asked the right questions or raised enough concern before its catastrophic implosion.

Black swans are such monumental events because of the level of disruption and impact to our lives. They happen suddenly and are largely unpredictable (at least before the fact). Bubbles occur when an insatiable demand leads people to chase pricing to ridiculous levels with a disregard for value or reason. Human psychology has not changed since the Tulip Mania. Experts continue to wrongly proclaim, "This time is different," and people continue throwing large sums of money away on things they don't fully understand.

Markets can stay irrational for a long time before correcting, and people always get hurt when they do. Crowd psychology is a powerful force, and it moves in both directions. When we adopt the herd mentality, we run with the bulls when things are good but risk being trampled when the stampede turns around. The only way to protect ourselves from black swans and bubbles is to keep our minds while others are losing theirs. When something seems too good to be true, it usually is. It is up to each of us to make sure we protect ourselves from unnecessary risks, invest wisely, and plan for the unexpected. With the proper mind-set, our hard-earned money can do magical things over time.

21

A Penny Saved Is a Penny Doubled

It's amazing how fast later comes
when you buy now.

—MILTON BERLE,
AMERICAN COMEDIAN
AND ACTOR

Preparing for the future requires us to recognize we will need money to pay for it when it gets here. Very few people need encouragement to spend their money. It's become a part of our culture. Everywhere we turn, we are bombarded by marketing ads showing us the latest and greatest things we should buy. We are encouraged to spend money to fuel our economy and makes ourselves feel good. The problem is that every dollar we spend today makes tomorrow much worse. Saving money, on the other hand, is the exact opposite. We sacrifice having something today in order to make tomorrow much better.

There is nothing immediately rewarding from living below our means and saving our money. In fact, it might even feel like a punishment to see those around us building bigger homes, driving fancier cars, and wearing more expensive brands. Meanwhile, we have no way of signaling to others our great success at planning for the future. For inspiration, I give you Warren Buffett, who happens to live just a few miles from me. I bet if I drove you through Warren's neighborhood, you couldn't pick out his home. It's the same one he bought for $31,500 in 1958.

One of the richest men in the world lives in one of the more modest houses on his street. He could literally buy whatever he wants, whenever he wants to, but even a billionaire understands that spending money isn't what creates happiness. "Really getting to do what you love to do every day—that's really the ultimate luxury," Buffett explains. "Your standard of living is not equal to your cost of living."

Many of us are unable to save enough money because we have chosen lifestyles we cannot afford. Unable to keep our expenses within reasonable limits, we have continued to increase spending as we have earned more. In today's culture we want a lot, and we want it now. We struggle to grasp the benefits of saving, and the costs of not saving, because we don't experience them until much later. As we learned earlier, we are lousy at being in touch with our future feelings. We can't emotionally connect with what financial security means for us later in life, but we sure know what that burst of happiness feels like when we blow money today.

Right now, we can't feel the horrible sting we will experience down the road when we cannot afford the things we expected to. Many of us will struggle to retire because we will still be paying for stuff we didn't need and hardly enjoyed. The whole point of working all these years isn't so we can keep making more money to spend; it's so we can have enough money to stop working!

I credit my dad for instilling a solid work ethic in me at a young age. Unfortunately, he also showed me how much fun it looked like he was having spending the money he made. Taking my cue from him, I worked long summers only to go back to college and blow my earnings on CDs, video games, clothes, and other things I barely used. With the money I wasted on things that added nothing to my happiness, I could have built a small fortune. Like so many other naïve people raised in the consumer economy, I hadn't yet appreciated the extremely powerful combination of time and money.

If I offered you either a million dollars in cash or the sum of a penny doubled every day for a month, which would you choose? The cool million sounds like a pretty safe bet until you realize a penny doubled for thirty days will be worth $10,737,418.24! This is the power of *compound interest,* or what Albert Einstein reportedly called the Eighth Wonder of the World. Benjamin Franklin described it best when he said, "Money makes money. And the money that makes money, makes money." It starts off so slowly we barely notice it happening. One penny turns into two pennies and then two pennies turn into four pennies. However, on the twenty-first day we make more than $5,000 and just ten days later we make more than 5 million dollars! Building wealth requires the discipline to save, the courage to invest, and the patience to leave it alone.

Although we obviously can't expect to double our money every single day for a month, we can use something called the *Rule of 72* to calculate a far more realistic return. Here's how the Rule of 72 works: If we know the current annual interest rate we expect to earn on an investment, we can divide 72 by that rate to determine how many years it will take to double our money. For example, if the stock market earns an average of 10 percent annually over the long term, then 72/10 = 7.2 years to double our investment. Therefore, if we invest $1,000 in the stock market when we are twenty-five years old, we can expect to have $2,000 when we are thirty-two.

But remember the magic of compound interest. Over the first 7.2 years, our initial $1,000 slowly doubled to $2,000. Now, that extra $1,000 we earned goes to work alongside the initial $1,000 we put in. This $2,000 will double over the next 7.2 years, giving us $4,000 when we turn thirty-nine. Carry this forward and we'll have $8,000 when we're forty-six, $16,000 when we're fifty-three, $32,000 when we're sixty, and $64,000 when we're sixty-eight and hopefully preparing for our retirement. This is a $64,000 pile of money generated solely from our initial $1,000 investment, without adding a single dollar to it ever again. Just imagine how big that pile would be if we continued to save and add little bits to this money machine all along the way?

Successful investors recognize that the truly significant gains don't happen immediately, which is why so many people these days find it difficult staying the course. We must maintain the discipline and patience to allow the process to play out. Routinely spending small sums of money is much easier than saving them, because we don't see them today for what they will eventually become. When we keep the concept of compound interest fresh in our minds, we can alter our daily habits and get our money to work for us. We can actually generate meaningful wealth just by making a few minor changes.

It became much easier for me once I began recognizing the *true* cost of today's purchases. For example, like millions of people, I used to stop and grab a $4 cup of coffee every morning. It was fairly easy to justify $4 on my way to work, plus by quickly scanning my auto-reloading mobile app, *I didn't even think about it*. It had become automatic.

I sat down and calculated that there are about 260 workdays in a year, so my automatic $4 morning coffee was actually costing me $1,040 every year. We know that $1,000 invested at age twenty-five is worth $64,000 at age sixty-eight. Therefore, if I am twenty-five years old, the true cost of my morning coffee habit is actually $64,000 for just one year, because I am forfeiting those future gains by spending the money now. Now, if I brew decent coffee at home instead at a cost of $240 a year, the remaining $800 invested would still be worth over $50,000! Again, this is only one year. Two years of this nets us over $100,000 and so on. Thinking in these terms enables us to make more prudent choices about the seemingly small purchases we don't think enough about.

In *Predictably Irrational,* Dan Ariely advises pulling the curtains back on our brains and routinely considering the true costs of what we spend our money on. We do this by training ourselves to regularly question our repeated behaviors. Morning coffee is a perfect example, but there are many others. Do we really need those subscriptions that are automatically charged and renewed? Do we pay for more television channels than we use? Do we actually read the papers and magazines delivered to us? What about memberships to country clubs, health clubs, swimming pools, or other facilities? How much is it really costing us per actual visit? Only by taking the time to examine where our money is actually going can we take control of what we want it to do for us.

The lowest-income households in the United States spend (on average) over $400 every year on lottery tickets. That is *four times* more than the wealthy spend on them. Perhaps it makes sense when we consider that the less fortunate are more desperate to chase a dream than those who are so much closer to living it. The big problem here is that 40 percent of Americans cannot come up with the same $400 in an emergency.

People are literally gambling their safety nets away chasing the million-to-one odds of hitting the jackpot. What if instead of throwing $400 away every year on lottery tickets, they continued investing it? They wouldn't have the millions of dollars they dreamed about, but they would most certainly be able to buy their way out of poverty. This, of course, assumes they have avoided drowning themselves in debt, which we will examine next.

Never spend your money before you have it.

—THOMAS JEFFERSON,
THIRD PRESIDENT
OF THE UNITED STATES

Businesses understand the flaws in our financial reasoning, and they continue innovating new methods for exploiting our weaknesses. For example, once companies have latched their recurring billings onto our credit cards, they become embedded like ticks. Credit cards are among the most effective tools of financial self-destruction ever created because they are so frequently misused. Credit cards should be used for only three primary purposes: as a convenient alternative to cash, as a way to generate free perks, and in case of emergency. That is all. If you don't pay your bill off every month (or soon after), you're just borrowing money at a high interest rate for every single item you charge on your card. Instead of saving and investing that money, you're throwing more of it away. It is the exact opposite of what we should be doing.

Credit card companies prey on our ignorance and lack of discipline, so it's critical to first understand just how unequal this relationship is. Let's say I am currently carrying a balance of $5,000 and the interest rate on my card is 20 percent. If I charge nothing else, it will still cost me $83 each month just to keep my balance from growing. Unless I pay more than $83, I get nowhere. Every single purchase I make on my credit card ends up costing much more than I expected at the time I made it. Often the great deal we got at the time of purchase ends up costing far more than the retail price once we finish paying for it. Adding insult to injury, we will often still be making payments on outdated styles and technology when updated versions are released. Credit cards make it easy for us to buy things right now, but we often remain on the hook long after. Meanwhile, our enthusiasm for most of what we buy tends to fade rather quickly.

But that isn't the really scary part. As wonderful as compound interest is when working in our favor, it is equally merciless when ballooning against us. It is the doubling penny in reverse! Each month, interest is charged on our unpaid credit card balances, raising the amount of money we owe. Then, the new money we owe from the interest itself begins accruing interest. If I can't at least cover the interest payments and stop using the card, my debt will continue snowballing higher. The Rule of 72 tells me that if my credit card has a 20 percent annual rate, and I can't keep up with the interest payments, my outstanding balance will double every 3.6 years. That initial $5,000 will soar to $20,000 in just over seven years. Credit card debt is a dangerous treadmill that speeds up faster and faster when we can't pay it off. Carrying a balance on a high-interest card can bury us financially.

Once we are clear about just how horrible an arrangement this is, there are steps we can take to get out of it. Let's begin by flipping the whole equation upside down. If I am currently stuck paying 20 percent annual interest on my credit card balance, then in a very real sense, every dollar I spend to pay down that balance is an automatic 20 percent annual return on my money! Where else am I going to find a guaranteed profit like that? Believe it or not, some people actually maintain stock portfolios and savings accounts while carrying credit card balances. Very few stocks and zero savings accounts will come anywhere close to offsetting a credit card balance with a high interest rate. These people are only falling further behind. All assets unlikely to generate a return higher than our credit card interest rate should be immediately sold and used to pay off our debt. It's the easiest money we will ever see.

Next, assuming I have been making regular monthly payments on my credit card, I likely have the kind of credit history other banks will salivate over. The ideal customer carries a balance and reliably pays the high interest rate every month. I'm a cash cow for them, and I should be able to find other cards with more favorable terms without much effort. Simply by transferring our balance from our current card charging us 20 percent, to a new card charging 15 percent, we've instantly "earned" ourselves 5 percent. This is good progress, but we aren't done since 15 percent is still an expensive loan. Also, beware of introductory low teaser rates that jump up after a short period of time. Make sure you understand the rules before you make the switch.

To recap: We sold our available assets to pay down our card balances and then switched to a new credit card with the lowest available interest rate. Now, for any balance still remaining, the next step is to immediately locate even cheaper money to pay it off. Ideally, we want to find bank loans, lines of credit, or mortgage refinancing options where we can borrow money below our new card's interest rate. For instance, if we can find a 10 percent interest loan to pay our remaining 15 percent card balance, we will net ourselves another immediate 5 percent "gain." We now have a new loan at half the interest rate we started with (10 percent versus our original 20 percent.) By slowing the compound interest machine from working so savagely against us, we now have a much more reasonable loan we can pay off. Once we do, we will finally be off the credit card treadmill for good, and get money working in our favor for a change.

By maintaining the discipline not to spend money we don't have, we can go on the offensive and beat credit card companies at their own game. The fierce competition for customers leads to valuable perks like cash-back bonuses, airline miles, executive club memberships, and other creative incentives. If I pay my balance in full every month, and my card pays a 2 percent cash-back bonus, I will actually make a free 2 percent profit on the money I've spent! If I charge a total of $20,000 per year on the card, that's a free $400 every year I can put to work growing my future rather than my debt. Now, by being in control of my finances, I'm literally earning both on money saved and on money spent.

If we are going to work for our money, we'd better make sure our money works for us. It takes time to grow, and the really exciting gains happen much later down the road. Starting early provides an advantage, but patience and consistency over a long period of time are essential. Prioritizing financial security over unnecessary spending explains why the wealthy don't always appear wealthy. When it comes to money, the smartest people I've met "grow it, don't show it." It also explains why some are able to weather the unexpected economic storms while others are tossed about in them.

Action Exercise

Record all of your expenses for at least one month. This is often a painful exercise, but it generates a lot of good information. Identify things you spend money on that you could easily do without. Use the Rule of 72 to calculate how much money you'd have in twenty years if you chose to invest that money instead.

22

Cleaning Out Our Closets

We are enriched not by what we possess,
but what we can do without.

—IMMANUEL KANT
GERMAN PHILOSOPHER

It is clear that our happiness level is impacted far greater by the things we choose to do rather than the things we choose to buy. Spending money now makes it harder for us to do more of what we want later. Today's financial discipline creates tomorrow's financial freedom, and tomorrow's financial freedom enables us to make more of our own choices in life. Many of the possessions we accumulate are like rocks added to a backpack. We rarely interact with them and they only slow our progress.

The more money we can free up to work for us, the more of it we can grow over time. This requires consistently making wise choices and remaining committed for the long term without being blown off course by our worst impulses. If we want to change our perspectives about spending money, we have to come to terms with how much of it we've wasted.

In order to save and invest our money, we have to live below our means. Yet many of us don't operate this way because we imagine ourselves assuming a degree of suffering and hardship other people aren't required to endure. To the contrary, our happiness levels actually increase dramatically once we begin acting more intelligently with our money. We will begin recognizing that the stuff we buy isn't actually making us happy now, and how it limits our ability to be happier later. To get there, we need to face some hard realities about why we bought some of the things we already have. Once we do, we will be conditioned to instinctively stop and question the actual benefit of a purchase before we pay for it. Prepare for an epiphany as you set a little time aside to take a thoughtful inventory of your possessions.

You may be familiar with the *Pareto Principle,* otherwise known as the *80/20 Rule.* The Pareto Principle can be reliably applied to countless situations where only a small percentage (20 percent) of the total actually accounts for the majority (80 percent) of the results. For example, in business we often see 20 percent of our customers accounting for 80 percent of the profits. In our leisure time, 20 percent of our music is often what we listen to 80 percent of the time. And despite all the clothes and accessories tucked away in our closets, drawers, and storage boxes, it's a safe bet we wear 20 percent of our wardrobe about 80 percent of the time.

When it comes to spotlighting our poor spending habits, we can begin by cleaning out our closets. We will identify many items we didn't need, don't wear, and shouldn't have bought in the first place. Working through our closets provides us with the financial intelligence we need to make many smarter decisions going forward.

If we truly only utilize 20 percent of the items in our closet, we shouldn't have to spend time every day sifting through the other 80 percent. Our goal is to isolate the items we actually reach for, and we do this by removing all the others we don't. Through this process, we are going to confront an important psychological hurdle called the *sunk cost fallacy,* which causes us to overvalue things solely because we spent our money on them. The reason we struggle to discard things is because when we make the actual decision to let go, we actively experience the loss of a wasteful purchase. It's called a *fallacy* because the real loss already occurred, back when we stopped using the item. The true test of something's value is not whether we paid for it, but whether or not we have been using it. Attachment and emotion have no role in this process.

From the 80/20 Rule, we now move on to a process I call the *One-Year Rule.* Basically, if we haven't worn something in the past year, we shouldn't have bought it in the first place, and don't need to keep it now. There are two exceptions to this rule: things we haven't worn because they currently don't fit and things we might need for sporadic occasions, such as ski pants or Kentucky Derby hats. These items should be boxed up and relocated to a storage area, so we don't need to buy them again when we need them.

With this in mind, we go through our wardrobe item by item and remove everything that hasn't been worn in the past year. Each item pulled will go into one of two piles: The "I will never wear this again" pile or the "I might actually wear this again" pile. When we are finished, our closets will contain only essential items. It may not seem like much, but guess what? That's all we've worn for an entire year!

Now we turn to the two piles we've made. The "I will never wear this again" pile contains everything we will be getting rid of immediately. Items in new or very good condition can often be sold on Internet sites like eBay or taken to a consignment store. This converts our unwanted items into ready cash to buy things we might actually wear, pay down a credit card, or save and invest. Whatever we can't sell can be donated to organizations like Goodwill or the Salvation Army, and we may even get a tax donation for doing so. Any benefit we can receive from discarding our unused clothing and accessories is far better than having them take up space and provide us with nothing of value.

The "I might actually wear this again" pile requires a little more thought. These are the items we aren't quite sure we are ready to part with just yet. What I do next is treat this pile like a shopping trip. Since I've already removed the items from my closet, I've dampened the impact of the sunk cost fallacy. Now I am forced to make a more objective decision on whether something deserves a place in my new wardrobe.

If I can commit to wearing it in the next month (weather permitting), I will hang it back up. If not, it gets boxed up and placed in storage. In six months, I will pull those boxes from storage and make a final decision on them. If I can commit to wearing them in the next month, they stay. Everything else gets sold or donated. I apply the One-Year Rule each spring, and it gets easier every year.

This process isn't limited to our clothing; any location where stuff is tucked away should be regularly evaluated for removal. I am embarrassed to say I have spent money on things only to realize I already had them in a drawer or cabinet somewhere. It is a sure sign we have too much stuff if we can't keep track of where we put it all. We spend far too much time in our living spaces to not know where our possessions are located. When was the last time you took a thorough inventory and removed some of the clutter at the same time?

Our closet is the ideal microcosm for our spending habits in general, and there should be a few powerful takeaways from this exercise. First, it becomes obvious we had more than we needed. We received no additional happiness from buying more things and, in fact, we will have freed up more valuable time by not having to sift through the same unused items every day. Second, we see how much money we spent without adequately considering how little benefit we would actually receive in return. The more we face these realities, the more conscientious we will be about our purchases going forward. Third, letting go of material possessions reinforces the importance of what really matters in our lives. The Japanese have a three-character word for this: *danshari,* which translates to severing a relationship with unnecessary things *(dan),* purging clutter that overwhelms the home *(sha),* and achieving a sense of peace by separating the self from things *(ri).*

Finally, the principle of quality is central to the three things that matter most in life: time, relationships, and money. We choose to invest much more of our time in fewer relationships because they are meaningful and long lasting. When we spread ourselves too thin, we have a larger number of lower-quality relationships with shallower connections. The same principle can be applied to our possessions. When we accumulate a greater number of inexpensive and poorly made goods, they will either fall apart quickly or go unused. However, when we invest a little more money in fewer quality items instead, we will receive a lot more benefit over time.

For example, some of the best clothing investments I ever made have been my relatively expensive leather dress shoes. I was apprehensive about spending so much more than I had in the past, but they were handmade with quality materials. I have worn them for over a decade now, including having them resoled multiple times, and they continue to age wonderfully. Compared to lesser-quality shoes that cost less but need to be replaced every two years, my "expensive" shoes have actually been a bargain! Price does not always reflect craftsmanship, but paying a little more for better quality often works out over time.

Cleaning out our closets is how we actively internalize the principle of *Less Is More*. Once we pare back to reveal the wardrobe we actually use, we can develop the financial intelligence to stop our habitual and needless shopping. A good tailor can alter and repair well-made clothing, and a good cobbler can repair well-made shoes. We should only buy things we expect to receive long-term value from. This is the essence of Marie Kondo's popular *KonMari Method,* which advocates tidying our possessions in order to live the lives we want. Our goal should be to keep everything that brings us joy and toss away everything else.

Action Exercise

Find a weekend to clean out your closets and work toward owning only things that add value. Use the One-Year Rule to declutter your living space and begin changing the way you think about spending money.

23

Fortune Favors the Prepared

*In preparing for battle, I have always found that
plans are useless, but planning is indispensable.*

—DWIGHT D. EISENHOWER,
FIVE-STAR ARMY GENERAL AND
THIRTY-FOURTH PRESIDENT
OF THE UNITED STATES

We have all observed other individuals
performing incredibly difficult tasks with
relative ease and thought to ourselves, "It isn't fair."
These include straight-A students who never have to
study, eloquent speakers who never refer to notes, and
star athletes who never have to train outside of practice.
There are rare prodigies who have been truly blessed
with extraordinary natural gifts the rest of us were not.
There are far more people who only appear to possess
these same innate abilities, but actually don't. They make
it appear effortless to us because we are totally unaware
of all the hard work put in behind the scenes. We see
only the results, not the years of preparation.

Preparation is commonly taken for granted, which
is why we toss around phrases like "overnight success
story," "rocket to stardom" and "next big thing." We typically assume stars appear out of nowhere because we are
completely ignorant of all the failures, persistence, and

struggles they endured along the way. We see a previously unknown actor suddenly appearing in multiple movies, a journeyman athlete now among the league leaders, and a quirky new company on magazine covers and advertisements.

What we didn't see was the actor waiting tables for years to pay bills while unsuccessfully auditioning for bit parts. We didn't see the athlete when he was cut from a previous team and worked out day and night to earn another chance. We didn't see the founders of the start-up company living in their cars to conserve capital while they built their dream. We celebrate the finished product without properly recognizing the monumental preparation it took to make it happen.

When you think of the early Beatles, you probably have an image of Beatlemania in the mid-1960s, when four handsome young lads from England suddenly took America by storm. Their toothy smiles and catchy pop songs catapulted them to instant superstardom. The reality is far different. In 1960, the boys went to Germany and played nearly 200 shows in small clubs for several hours a night. Living together in squalid conditions, they were completely devoted to each other and to playing music. This period was not glamorous, but it was vital for sharpening their skills, tightening their cohesiveness, and strengthening their songwriting.

When they returned to England, they had become the most experienced rock band on the planet. The Fab Four may have suddenly burst onto the scene in the eyes of the world, but that view diminishes the importance of the years spent diligently preparing as unknown musicians. Paying our dues in the shadows is what prepares us for the eventual spotlights.

When it comes to our money and our careers, we must be consistently prepared for each opportunity we encounter. Preparation affects our performances in interviews. It affects the quality of our work, how we are evaluated, and the degree to which we will advance. Most importantly, it affects our ability to project confidence. When we invest the time to prepare, we make our performance appear effortless. As a result, we are viewed as capable of handling increased responsibilities. Being unprepared, on the other hand, leaves the impression of being unreliable and easily overwhelmed.

Leaders are able to confidently make quick decisions in stressful situations because they have already worked through potential scenarios in advance. They are not left to guess or gamble when the pressure is on. Preparation should be viewed as a priority, not an inconvenience. Remember: We never know who is watching. Being prepared at the right time can change our lives. Unfortunately, being unprepared at the wrong time can change our lives, too, as the following story makes clear.

A terrible storm engulfed a small town, and the downpour soon turned into a flood. As the waters rose, the local preacher knelt in prayer on the church porch. Soon, a man came paddling down the street in a canoe.

"Get in, Preacher. This rain isn't letting up."

"I will trust in the Lord," said the preacher. "If I am in danger, He will help me."

As the water continued rising, the preacher climbed up on the church balcony, when another man passed by on a motorboat.

"Take my hand, Preacher. We need to get you out of here. The levee won't hold much longer."

Once again, the preacher was unmoved. "I shall remain. The Lord will see me through."

Eventually, the levee broke, and only the church steeple remained above water. The preacher was up there, clinging to the cross, when a helicopter descended from the clouds and the pilot shouted to him through a megaphone.

"Climb up this ladder, Preacher. You're almost out of time."

Undeterred, the preacher shouted back, "Please save someone else. The Lord will take care of me."

Soon after, he drowned.

In Heaven, the preacher met God and asked Him, "Lord, my faith in you never wavered. Why did you let that flood swallow me up?"

God shook his head. "Let's see, Preacher, I sent you a canoe, a motorboat, and a helicopter. What else would you have liked me to do?"

As the preacher learned all too well, hope is not a strategy. Proper preparation is a strategy with three steps: gather the best information we can attain at the time, identify the potential outcomes, and determine our next moves for each outcome. Once we've done this, we are adequately prepared unless new information becomes available. If it does, we then go through this process again to evaluate whether our next moves remain the most prudent. Our plans must always reflect the reality as it is now, not what it once was or what we wish it would be. History is littered with failed leaders who refused to acknowledge and meet the challenges of new realities.

Without question, the most valuable aspect of my legal education was being frequently forced to argue positions I didn't necessarily agree with. It trained me to evaluate the strengths and weaknesses of opposing viewpoints and be prepared to defend either side. Knowing our opponents' vulnerabilities, as well as our own, is the essence of preparation. In 1854, another attorney, named Abraham Lincoln, sat down and wrote out the arguments for and against slavery. He needed to understand both sides clearly in order to test his views against the best arguments he was likely to face. This was how he gathered information.

With the Internet at our fingertips, we can gather information so much more easily than Lincoln could, yet it still shocks me how many people waste these easy opportunities. For example, with a scheduled phone call or meeting with someone new, why wouldn't we take five minutes to research the person first? A quick social media check might reveal common interests, hobbies, favorite restaurants, or sports teams. Doing a little homework can provide us with potential questions or topics of conversation to keep in our pockets, ultimately putting us in a much more comfortable frame of mind. Often the small details make the biggest difference, and they take very little time to obtain.

Let's say we have a client meeting next week to discuss the renewal of our contract. As part of our preparation, we should compile a list of the many instances when we've provided valuable services and contributed to our client's success. We should be well versed on our advantages over our competitors to defend our pricing structure. We should also internally review any of our own shortcomings and expect our client to bring them up. Once we've gathered this information, we will be far better prepared to confidently discuss the strengths and weaknesses of our position.

Next, we should anticipate the likely scenarios we will face. In our example, there are three main possibilities: our client will renew the contract, our client will want to renegotiate the contract, or our client will not renew the contract.

Obviously the latter two scenarios are not ideal for us, but we will not be blindsided by either one because we will be prepared. We know our client may have an enticing proposal from a competitor, and we can defend our advantages against it. We have reviewed all situations where we may have disappointed the client, and we can readily explain how we have made amends. Whatever direction the meeting takes, we will be well informed enough to competently handle each potential scenario.

Once again, there is no benefit in excessively worrying about what might happen. We know what might happen, and we will have given reasoned thought to how we will respond in those situations. Things do not always turn out the way we planned, but we can only deal with our reality as it exists right now. Hope is not a strategy, but neither is panic. *Remember:* We must focus only on what we can control, and we must always remain open to new information. A solid plan is also adaptable for when the conditions have actually changed.

Unfortunately, no matter how much preparation we put in, we can never completely control the outcome. There will always be unpredictable variables. In 1996, boxer Evander Holyfield was a serious underdog in his upcoming bout with the champion, Mike Tyson. Despite the long odds against him, Holyfield had been confidently sharing with reporters the strategy he'd employ to win the fight. When Tyson was asked if he was worried about Holyfield's fight plan, he famously replied, "Everybody has a plan until they get punched in the mouth." It was a humorous take on a classic military axiom: "No plan survives first contact with the enemy." Every strategy should be thoughtfully considered, but we must expect the unexpected. Only a fool thinks he has a foolproof plan.

Thanks to his preparation, Holyfield did survive being punched in the mouth to pull a huge upset in his first fight with Tyson. Their rematch was a case study in how a lack of preparation can lead to disaster. From the opening bell, Holyfield thoroughly dominated Tyson, who quickly became frustrated and lost his composure. After only three rounds, the fight was stopped when Tyson bit off a chunk of Holyfield's ear! Tyson was thoroughly unprepared and unable to adapt to what he encountered in the ring, resulting in his embarrassing breakdown and disqualification.

I suffered my own embarrassing professional blunder due to a complete lack of preparation on my part. At the time, I was eager to leave option trading and return to the business world. A commercial real estate broker I had known for years approached me with an intriguing idea. He made a persuasive argument for starting a property management—only company that did not do any brokerage deals. It sounded exciting, so I obtained my real estate license and we got to work. We began knocking on doors and setting up meetings to pitch our revolutionary business model and below-market pricing. We quickly secured a decent-sized client through an existing relationship, and it seemed we would be off and running. We were running, all right, but only in circles. It didn't take long before all the mistakes I had made became clear.

In my excitement to start a new company, I deliberately avoided gathering some important information I had access to. I relied completely on my partner's enthusiasm and experience, without doing my own research. I knew a few successful real estate people in the area, but I naïvely avoided reaching out to them because I didn't want to tip them off that we'd soon be competitors.

It turns out they were never concerned about us at all. In fact, one told me he wished he could have shown me why our business model was a mistake. The reason our company didn't already exist is because property management divisions weren't operated as profit centers. They were value-added services for the brokerage side, which is where the smart companies actually made their money. Oops.

To sum up: I started a company focused on the least profitable aspect of the real estate industry and deliberately ignored the most profitable! I could easily have learned this sooner, but I buried my head in the sand so I wouldn't have to face any negativity. But that wasn't all. Not only was I guilty of willful ignorance, but I was also negligently unprepared. I never took the time to plan out the finances of the business ahead of time. If I had worked up a simple business plan, it would have been clear that the business relied entirely on two people (us!) actively managing properties full time. In order to grow, we needed to hire managers, which would eat up our profits, and our below-market prices didn't exactly help.

By not properly preparing, I found myself trapped in a cage I could never work my way out of. As one of only two managers, I would always be working in the business rather than on the business. More problematic was discovering that the business was simply not scalable. We would need additional properties in order to grow, and each manager had limited capacity. We could never grow our profits enough to offset the costs of hiring additional people. We didn't even need to worry about growing, however. Because we had failed to perform the proper market research in advance, it wasn't long before we discovered the overwhelming lack of enthusiasm for a cheap, unproven management company that owners would be willing to trust their buildings with.

Proper preparation would have saved me from learning this costly lesson. I did not properly gather information or anticipate possible scenarios. This was a failure, to be sure, but I was determined to learn a few things from it. I now seek out advice when it is available, and I don't worry about the potential of someone stealing a great idea. Great ideas only become great businesses when they are executed by great people. If my only competitive advantage is being first, it probably is not a sustainable business in the long term.

Once the reality became clear, I exited the partnership. I might have failed to prepare, but at least I changed course when I finally received new information. The three steps of proper preparation can save us from a lot of mistakes, particularly when it comes to money. My property management business was a preventable failure, but it was not a disaster because I learned from it. This is an example of failure teaching us far more than our successes can, as we will explore next.

Action Exercise

Make preparation a priority. Take out your journal and actively prepare for your important conversations and meetings. Gather the available information and anticipate the possible scenarios. Afterward, go back and grade yourself on how prepared you were.

24

Failing to Succeed

You got to lose to know how to win.

—STEVEN TYLER,
LEAD SINGER OF AEROSMITH
IN *DREAM ON*

One of the biggest misconceptions about successful people is that they got there by avoiding mistakes and failures. The reality is, more often than not, they were forced to overcome stumbles, hardships, and misfortunes along the way. Consider President Lincoln again, widely revered as the only man great enough to preserve the Union and end slavery during the worst period in our nation's history. His masterful leadership during the Civil War demonstrated an expert blend of wisdom and political shrewdness. However, little is known about the string of failures that prepared him for his monumental undertaking. Chip Conley provides us with the perfect summary from *Emotional Equations:*

> When Abraham Lincoln was 7, he and his family were forced out of their home and he had to start working to help support his parents. When he was 9, his mother died. As a child, he was kicked in

the head by a horse, and once he nearly drowned. Throughout his life, he suffered from malaria (twice), syphilis, and smallpox. At age 21, he failed in business. At age 23, he ran for the state legislature, lost his job, and was turned down for law school. That same year, he started another business on borrowed money, but a year later he was bankrupt. At age 26, he was engaged to be married but his fiancée died; soon afterward, his only sister died during childbirth. Lincoln hit an emotional low and took to his bed for six months.

At age 28, he was defeated as speaker of the state legislature. At age 33, he ran for the U.S. House of Representatives and lost. He tried again at age 39 and lost again. He ran for the U.S. Senate at age 45 and lost. He tried for his party's vice-presidential nomination at age 47 and lost. And lost again for the U.S. Senate at age 49. Despite all this, at age 52, Abraham Lincoln was elected the 16th president of the United States.

Any one of these setbacks alone would be reason enough for despair, but imagine having to endure them all. What we've learned about failure is that Lincoln did not become president "despite all this," he became president "because of all this." The battery of obstacles he faced throughout his life didn't impede his progress, they strengthened it. Failure is our greatest teacher, and we must learn to embrace the opportunities to overcome our disappointments. Only by working through letdowns are we able to emerge smarter, stronger, and more experienced. Avoiding failure is avoiding growth, and without growth there is no success. Lincoln could easily have lost his confidence, his motivation, or even his will to continue living. Thankfully, he continued building his character and wisdom with each setback he encountered. The country would eventually need every bit of it during its darkest hours.

Failing to Succeed

You don't drown by falling in the water;
you drown by staying there.

—EDWIN LOUIS COLE,
AMERICAN MINISTER

Earlier we established the importance of developing confidence and being willing to face rejection. When we are rejected, we can hold our head up because all we've lost is the opportunity. When we fail, however, we had the opportunity to prove ourselves and we came up short. We have evidence to support our feelings of unworthiness and embarrassment. Still, we must be willing to accept failure if we plan on improving in any meaningful way. When we avoid challenges to protect ourselves from the pain of disappointment, we are laying the groundwork for a life filled with regrets and broken dreams. The path to success always takes us through difficulties and hardships. They are often our best teachers. As Dale Carnegie put it, "The most important thing in life is to profit from your losses because any fool can capitalize on their gains."

In her 2013 Harvard commencement speech, Oprah Winfrey told graduates to "learn from every mistake, because every experience and encounter, particularly your mistakes, are there to teach you and force you into being more of who you are." She added this incredible insight: "There is no such thing as failure; failure is just life trying to move us in another direction." Although it can be demoralizing to feel we weren't good enough, we can find inspiration from the many famous people who were actually moved toward their successes as a result of failing.

After graduating from college, Warren Buffett took an eleven-hour train ride to interview with the Harvard Business School, where he was turned down in just ten minutes. This forced him to attend Columbia instead, where he met his mentor, Benjamin Graham. Had Buffett been accepted to Harvard, he might never have become one of the richest men in the world.

Even though Anderson Cooper graduated from Yale, he couldn't even get an interview for a job at ABC answering phones and making copies. This forced him to go out and develop himself as a news correspondent, which is the role ABC eventually hired him for. "As it turned out, not getting that entry-level job there was the best thing that ever happened to me," he said. Had he actually been hired for the position he originally wanted, we likely wouldn't even know his name. He later left ABC to join CNN, where he was then fired from his morning show. Cooper refused to be defeated and fought his way back on the air by filling in as an anchor for every available time slot he could. Eventually he became one of the network's biggest stars. Throughout his career, Anderson Cooper's failures moved him closer to his calling, and overcoming the adversity he faced is what shaped him.

In studying the various paths of many successful individuals, I've noticed one recurring theme: Many of them single out "fear of failure" as the greatest limitation they see in others. Successful people celebrate working through their most distressing moments as the catalyst to their growth. Like so many others, they, too, were scared and discouraged, but they refused to give up. This determination, more than anything else, is the reason we know their stories.

Abraham Lincoln's road to the presidency was unimaginable, but he wasn't the only politician to find success in the wake of crushing losses. After serving as vice president of the United States for two terms, Richard Nixon went on to lose both the presidential election and the California gubernatorial election in the span of just two years. Many were convinced this one-two punch would end his political career. A dejected Nixon was even quoted telling reporters, "You don't have Nixon to kick around anymore, because, gentlemen, this is my last press conference." But they certainly would, because Tricky Dick dusted himself off and spent the next few years rebuilding his image. He channeled the lessons from his failures into his biggest success when he was elected president in 1968.

You may have heard of the critically acclaimed band Wilco, or its front man, Jeff Tweedy, but you may not be as familiar with Uncle Tupelo. Tweedy formed Uncle Tupelo with his friend Jay Farrar in high school, and they released four albums together. Just as they seemed on the verge of a breakout, Farrar suddenly broke up the band without explanation. A demoralized Tweedy could easily have given up on his music career. Instead, he picked up the broken pieces and started over with no idea his next band, Wilco, would be a huge success. As he reflects in his autobiography, "The people who seem the most like geniuses are not geniuses. They're just more comfortable with failing. They try more and they try harder than other people, and so they stumble onto more songs." Tweedy stumbled onto a Grammy award and nominations in four different genres over the next two decades. Had Uncle Tupelo not imploded, Tweedy might only have been known as a member of a popular bar band. Working through failure lifted him to extraordinary creative heights.

John Paul Dejoria was fired three times by beauty companies before he cofounded Paul Mitchell. To get his company going, he borrowed $350 from his mom to invest in the business, and he lived in his car on $2.50 a day. Once Paul Mitchell became a huge success, he went on to start the Patrón Spirits Company. Few people are able to launch one incredibly successful business, but to have two of them in wildly different industries is an extremely rare feat. Like other successful individuals, Dejoria credits hard work and overcoming failure for his accomplishments. "Things that appear to be setbacks at the time often end up being for the best," he said.

Stories like these have inspired me throughout the years as I worked my way through setbacks of my own. I have failed and started over multiple times. Throughout college and law school I had been preparing to join my dad's swimming pool business, only to quickly realize it was not what I wanted. Until then, I had failed to explore any other career I might have been interested in. I then moved my life to Omaha and joined Carl, my father-in-law, in his packaging business. When he sold the company four years after I arrived, I became an options trader, commuting back to Chicago during the workweeks for a year. After that didn't work out, I leaped into the property management business without properly preparing for it. From there, I returned to the packaging industry, where I applied lessons learned from these various experiences to find success. But not before having to overcome my biggest failure of all.

After decades spent building a successful packaging distribution company, Carl came out of retirement to start a new business from scratch with me. Noncompete agreements prevented us from hiring people we wanted, and customer contracts prevented us from growing the business as quickly as we hoped. These limitations contributed to our foolishly hiring someone without doing a thorough background check. In just over a year, this individual dragged us into financial and legal land mines we could never have imagined. This was without a doubt the scariest and most stressful period in my life, but it was also when I experienced the most professional growth.

Navigating this quagmire taught me some very important lessons. First and foremost, few things feel worse than being responsible for losing other people's money, particularly someone you care about. Our business was in so much trouble at one point that we couldn't get a bank loan and we couldn't sell the business. There was nowhere for me to hide from the pressure; my father-in-law was constantly stressed out, which meant my wife was constantly stressed out. I felt the weight of the entire family on my shoulders every day.

I also learned you never know what you are made of until your back is against the wall. There were no lifelines to grab onto and panic wasn't going to help. Nor was feeling sorry for myself. I realized the only two options were to close the business or to find a way to turn it around. The first thing we needed to do was stop the financial bleeding, so we pared back all expenses and focused our investments only on the best people and profitable business. It took time for the lingering issues to get resolved, but we began to see real progress. My confidence strengthened as I saw the plan take hold. I had helped steer the ship away from the iceberg.

I had proven my ability to run a packaging company and brought us back to breakeven. With profitability now in the forecast, I had been in discussions with banks and private equity investors for future support. At this point, Carl made the decision to sell the majority of our business to another packaging company, where I became a minority owner. After all I felt I had accomplished in bringing us back from the brink, and with so much growth on the horizon, it was a devastating blow for me. Fortunately, all I had learned through my challenges paid off as I earned a key role with my new parent company and a terrific group of colleagues to work with. It wasn't exactly what I expected or wanted, but it worked out better than I could have hoped.

There were many sleepless nights Stacey and I were genuinely worried about our future. At times I felt trapped, like I had wasted way too much of my past to achieve what I wanted in the future. Now, I believe all the different experiences better prepared me for what was to come. I believe I succeeded because I was able to focus only on what I could control, and I learned from every failure. Like Ian Schrager and Abraham Lincoln, I put one foot in front of the other and kept moving forward. The reason people give up is because they tend to look at how far they still have to go instead of how far they have come.

Lastly, my decisions throughout my career taught me another very important lesson: If you don't earn it, it's not really yours. There is a big difference between receiving assistance and having everything given to us. Marcus Aurelius said, "A person needs to stand on their own, not be propped up." When we rely upon other people for support, we have sacrificed our independence. When our promotion is due more to a relationship than to our merits, we don't deserve the position. Not only will we struggle to earn the respect of our coworkers but we will also be deprived of the feelings of pride and accomplishment necessary for our happiness. I worked in two family businesses and I can tell you there is no greater feeling than proving your own value and standing on your own two feet. As fashion photographer Bill Cunningham said, "If you don't take money, they can't tell you what to do, kid."

Money: Summary

Understanding where money fits into the three things that matter most is vital to our happiness in life. Refer to the Venn diagram as a reminder that money is the smallest of the three circles. If money were really more important than time, we would be happier than ever. But we aren't. As Morgan Housel explains, "Compared to generations prior, control over your time has diminished. And since controlling your time is such a key happiness influencer, we shouldn't be surprised that people don't feel much happier even though we are, on average, richer than ever." No amount of money can compete with choosing how we spend our time.

As for money and relationships, we see the same dynamic. Sociologist Karl Pillemer interviewed a thousand elderly Americans in order to compile the biggest lessons they'd learned in their lives. Guess what? Not a single one said it's important to be as wealthy as the people around us. What was truly important to them were quality friendships and quality time with family.

Therefore, it is clear that having more money will increase our well-being only when it enables us to control our time and enjoy our relationships. That is the sweet spot where the three circles overlap on the diagram. More money at the expense of time or relationships is a net loss to our well-being.

- The more money we have, the more we tend to isolate ourselves from others. The degradation of personal connections is directly correlated with unhappiness and depression.

- Money is important, but only to cover our needs and protect us from emergencies. Having more money does not equate to more happiness.

- Our views about money are corrupted by our perspectives. Most people erroneously feel they need more than they have because they compare themselves to others.

- Spending money on experiences is always a better value than spending money on things.

- Black swan events are outliers nobody thought possible, carry an extreme impact, and seem predictable in retrospect.

- Living beyond our means is a recipe for disaster and paralyzes our ability to survive unforeseen hardships and black swans.

- We must be prepared for black swan events because most experts are caught off guard by them.

- Bubbles in pricing have come and gone since the 17th century. The herd mentality will never go away, and we must be smart to avoid being trampled by it.

- Saving and investing our money takes discipline and time, but it is the surest path to long-term wealth.

- Compound interest: our money makes money, and that money makes more money. Every dollar spent today on things we don't need ends up costing a lot more tomorrow.

- Credit card debt is financial self-destruction. Paying it off and getting rid of high interest loans should be a high priority.

- We have to understand all the things we are wasting money on in order to change our perspective about spending money. Cleaning out our closets is one of the best ways to internalize the principle of Less Is More.

- Preparing for each opportunity we face is the most important habit we can develop.

- Overnight success stories are usually years in the making.

- Proper preparation involves gathering the best information we can attain at the time, identifying the potential outcomes, and determining our next moves for each outcome

- We should make proper preparation a habit for every upcoming conversation and meeting of any importance. Never waste an opportunity to gather information.

- Preparation is essential, but so is adapting to changing circumstances. Remember: "Everybody has a plan until they get punched in the mouth."
- Failure is our best teacher.
- Most successful individuals had to overcome failures along the way. Working through setbacks and overcoming disappointment shapes us for our eventual successes.
- If you don't earn it, it's not yours. There is no self-fulfillment in having money or a career handed to you.

In Closing:
Putting It All Together

What a wonderful life I had!
I only wish I had realized it sooner.

—COLETTE,
FRENCH AUTHOR

If only we could transport ourselves way into the future and look back on our time here, we would certainly find it easier to make better decisions. Three of the most common regrets expressed by those nearing the end of their lives include not doing the things they wanted to, not fully appreciating the people they cared about, and working too hard. In other words, they regret wasting the three things that matter most. How we prioritize our time, relationships, and money while we have them will determine how we feel when it's time for us to say good-bye. The more opportunities we have to link the three of them together, the more fulfilling our life experiences will be.

Time is not unlimited and there is no going back. We must spend it wisely on what we feel is meaningful. How we value our relationships, both with ourselves and with those close to us, determines a major portion of our happiness. Lastly, very few people look back and regret

213

having too little money; plenty deeply regret working too hard for it.

Leo Tolstoy's 1886 novella *The Death of Ivan Ilych* tells the story of a Russian judge at the end of an unremarkable life largely spent climbing social and professional ladders. Married to a wife he despises and children he has little connection to, Ilych meets his end incapacitated at home with a terminal illness. After chastising God for tormenting him so terribly in his final days, Ilych hears a voice ask him what it is he wants. "Why, to live as I used to," he replies, "well and pleasantly." It was only when hearing himself say those words that Ilych realized he hadn't actually lived well or pleasantly. In fact, everything following his childhood memories had been a long slide downward. "Maybe I did not live as I ought to have done," it suddenly occurred to him. "But how could that be, when I did everything properly?" "Properly" to Ilych meant focusing all his time on improving his status. As a result, he lived a life devoid of meaningful relationships and happiness. And now it had come to an end. Take a moment and consider how you might answer if that same voice asked you, "What do you want?"

I want to close with a very real and very recent example of time running out on me. When Stacey and I left Chicago years ago, we said good-bye to a group of very close friends and had to start all over making new relationships in Omaha. The very first couple we met, Steven and Carrie, had just moved from Canada and became dear friends of ours immediately. We traveled together, shared major holidays together, and our children grew up together. As I approached the end of writing this book, they informed us they were moving back to Canada in just a couple of weeks.

We had always assumed that this was a possibility for them one day, but it was a huge shock to us nonetheless. I immediately went through all the videos and pictures from the seventeen years we had shared, and I was overcome by the magnitude of what would soon be leaving our lives. Even more painful was my regret over how little time we had spent together the past few years and how much we took their proximity to us for granted. With our children at different schools, we chose to spend too much time with too many people who could never mean to us what Carrie and Steven did. And now that time was gone.

I have grown accustomed to the mind-set that the world is unpredictable and that we can never forecast the future with complete certainty. And yet, I still failed myself by not applying the three things that matter most to two of my closest friends. I wasted plenty of time that could have been spent on a meaningful relationship, and now I've lost that time and my ability to make up for it. With that in mind, I ask one last question: What matters most to you right now?

Action Exercise

Yes, you've reached the end of the book but please do not put it on the shelf just yet. The real value in this material is unlocked by implementing the concepts I've shared with you, not just reading about them. Your final action exercise is to review all the action exercises and put them to work! If you have any questions or comments, I would love to hear them! Feel free to e-mail me: brettatlas@mac.com.

Recommended Reading

The following books helped generate and develop many of the ideas you just read. They run the gamut from biography, history, philosophy, and psychology. If my house burned down, these would be the first books I would replace (sadly, my highlighting and notes would be lost).

Fantasyland (2017), Kurt Anderson, Penguin Random House LLC

Predictably Irrational (2008), Dan Ariely, HarperCollins

Emotional Equations (2012), Chip Conley, Simon & Schuster

Flow: The Psychology of Optimal Experience (1990), Mihaly Csikszentmihalyi, Harper Perennial

Stumbling on Happiness (2006), Daniel Gilbert, Random House, Inc.

What Got You Here Won't Get You There: How Successful People Become Even More Successful (2007), Marshall Goldsmith, Hyperion

Sapiens (2015), Yuval Noah Harari, HarperCollins

The Daily Stoic (2016), Ryan Holiday, Portfolio/Penguin

The Psychology of Money (2020), Morgan Housel, Harriman House

Rejection Proof (2015), Jia Jang, Harmony Publishing

Tribe: On Homecoming and Belonging (2016), Sebastian Junger, Hachette Book Group

The Biggest Bluff: How I Learned to Pay Attention, Master Myself, and Win (2020), Maria Konnikova, Penguin Press

Extraordinary Popular Delusions and the Madness of Crowds, Charles Mackay, Richard Bentley London

The Subtle Art of Not Giving a F*ck (2016), Mark Manson, HarperOne

Factfulness (2018), Hans Rosling with Ola Rosling and Anna Rosling Rönnlund, Flatiron Books

The Order of Time (2017), Carlo Rovelli, Riverhead Books

Behave (2017), Robert M. Sapolsky, Penguin Random House LLC.

Being Wrong (2010), Kathryn Schulz, HarperCollins

Getting There (2015), Gillian Zoe Segal, Abrams Image

The Elephant in the Brain (2018), Kevin Simler and Robin Hanson, Oxford University Press

The Black Swan (2007), Nassim Nicholas Taleb, Random House

The Death of Ivan Ilych (1886), Leo Tolstoy

About the Author

Brett Atlas is a Senior Vice President and shareholder of MJS Packaging, a 135-year-old container distributor headquartered in Livonia, Michigan. He also has owned businesses in several different industries, including construction, distribution, finance, technology, and real estate.

A licensed attorney, Brett is a graduate of The John Marshall Law School in Chicago, Illinois. He received a bachelor of science in business from the University of Kansas in Lawrence.

Brett is a senior contributor for Bourbon & Banter, a popular Internet blog for bourbon enthusiasts. Originally from Chicago, Illinois, Brett now lives in Omaha, Nebraska, with his wife and three children. He invites feedback from readers at: **brettatlas@mac.com.**